THE JOY OF WATER

CONTENTS

INTRODUCTION

Wherever my wanderings take me around the globe, big city to remote backcountry, I have a few things I need to do to feel I have truly experienced a destination.

One of these is to swim: in whatever body of water that place presents me with.

When I lived in North London, it was often a de-stressing dunk in one of the ponds scattered across Hampstead Heath. On work trips to Budapest, a near obligation was soaking in the thermal baths for which that city is renowned. And hiking across northwest Scotland, however icy the temperature, a plunge off a lonely beach like Sandwood Bay made an outing there complete.

It was not for bravado or to honour some rite of passage that I felt this need. It was as if by indulging in these wild swims I was wallowing in that place's primordial essence; delving as deep into its soul as was possible. Climbers go through something similar, as do cavers, as do divers: ascending or descending so far that a different world starts to envelop them. Yet a dip in our planet's waters rarely requires specialist equipment, save perhaps some gumption. And once immersed, it is an absolute sensory experience: you smell it, you hear it, it touches every inch of you. It is the easiest way to throw yourself into nature's great unknowns.

Surveys show similar findings. A 2013 study on happiness in natural environments, conducted by professors at a couple of British universities, collated responses from 20,000 participants in varying locations and found coastal and marine environments aroused the greatest joy of any. History concurs. For centuries we have been going to the seaside, taking to the waters at spas or splashing in rivers and lakes for our well-being. When we are around water, it tends to bring us out in smiles and often in shrieks of laughter.

The 68 watery locales featured in this book will conjure other emotions beside elation. On the dreamy beaches of Mozambique's Bazaruto Archipelago, it could be pure peace. Healing properties in mineral waters at Bad Gastein in Austria purportedly cure certain ailments. Snorkelling Australia's Ningaloo Reef, you might feel sheer awe at the diverse surrounding sea life.

These places will hopefully whet your appetite for all things aquatic. But this book has another aim: to raise awareness of the best spots to enjoy water, our most precious resource, so that they are preserved for future generations.

The book is divided into five chapters by continent: Africa, the Americas, Asia, Europe and Oceania. Readers can discover new places in each part of the world to splash in, soak up or simply stare out at the water, as well as remembering places they have already been – and hope to return to. ~ **Luke Waterson**

© THPStock | Getty Images

AFRICA

ANSE SOURCE D'ARGENT

Pick your patch of sand along an achingly beautiful, boulder-strewn beach commonly named among the world's top 10.

Stumbling onto the most famous beach in the Seychelles, it's easy to see why no 'best beaches' round-up would be complete without this Indian Ocean stunner. Lapped by crystal-clear tropical water, this pristine strip of sand lined by craning coconut palms and huge granite boulders on the small island of La Digue seems almost too beautiful to be real.

While there are some guesthouses on La Digue, most people visit on a day trip from neighbouring Praslin. You can walk the 2.7km (1.7 miles) to the beach from the marina, but renting a bike will give you more time at the beach. Unless you want to walk through the water, you'll need to pass through L'Union Estate coconut plantation to reach the beach (hence the fee), but it's oh-so-worth-it for a day of paradisiacal beach lazing.

Country Seychelles • **Region** La Digue Island • **Type** beach • **Cost** Rs115 • **Family friendly** yes

Rent a bike to get around ~
Jump in a boat to explore
~ Discover sandy nooks ~
The stunning Seychelles

Can I snorkel off the beach?
Only at high tide. There are plenty of rock pools to explore when the tide goes out.

How far along the shoreline can I safely explore?
Keep walking past the main beach and you'll find lots of little sandy nooks between the boulders that line the shore. A dry bag can come in handy for your valuables, as the rocky shore can be slippery. Travellers with sensitive feet may be more comfortable in reef shoes.

Can I buy lunch here?
You can purchase drinks at a cute little beach bar at the far end of the sandy pathway alongside the beach, but if you're not staying on the island you're best off bringing a packed lunch from Praslin as there aren't many places to eat nearby.

Is there anything else to see on La Digue?
Don't miss the pen of Aldabra giant tortoises in L'Union Estate.

Anse Marron

Reached by a challenging hike to the island's southern tip, Anse Marron is another incredible beach worth seeking out on La Digue. The island also plays home to the critically endangered Seychelles paradise flycatcher, of which there are only 100 left.

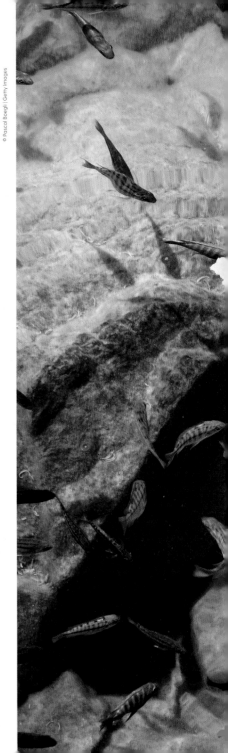

CAPE MACLEAR

Put down your Malawi gin and pick up your snorkel for a boat trip out to Thumbi Island to swim with brightly coloured cichlid fish.

The lazy and lovely village of Cape Maclear is one of Lake Malawi's most laid-back and scenic spots. You may find it hard to prise yourself off the golden sands to do anything, but a boat trip across to the pyramidal wooded island of Thumbi is well worth the effort. Lake boatmen will take you just offshore, from where you can don goggles or a snorkel and ease yourself into the balmy lake waters. A swim round the rocks at Thumbi quickly reveals the cichlid fish for which the lake is famous.

The little cichlid themselves may not offer the wow factor and visual diversity that you get on a coral reef adventure, but their colours dazzle – watching these amber yellow, fuchsia pink, orange, indigo and turquoise creatures dart around you as you dip is a rare delight.

Country Malawi • **Region** Southern Malawi • **Type** lake • **Website** www.capemaclear.org • **Cost** US$30 for 2 to 4 people • **Activities** boat trip • **Family friendly** yes

Strap on a snorkel and be dazzled by colourful cichlid fish

How are the views?
Gorgeous: clear blue waters dotted with wooden dugout canoes, edged with golden sand and ringed by densely forested hills.

Tell me about Lake Malawi
The third-largest and second-deepest lake in Africa, Lake Malawi is a vast stretch of glorious fresh water which links Malawi with neighbours Mozambique to the east and Tanzania to the north.

Is the water safe?
Yes, but don't swim after dark because that's when hippos come to the shore. And all visitors to the lake should have a bilharzia test six weeks after their last lake swim. The disease – an infection caused by parasitic worms – is very easily cured, but dangerous if left untreated.

How do I get here?
Cape Maclear lies down a (partially) bumpy track from Monkey Bay – you can arrange a pickup from the turn-off or take a motorbike taxi. Other options include taxis from Blantyre or Lilongwe, and boat transfers from Senga Bay.

Cichlid Species

Lake Malawi supports 850 to 1000 cichlid species – more freshwater species than in all of Europe. Known as *mbuna* locally, the fish exemplify Darwin's theory of adaptive radiation, where a species explodes into related but divergent forms. Careful parents, cichlid protect eggs and fry in their mouths until their offspring can cope alone.

BAZARUTO ARCHIPELAGO

Sail away to a pristine tropical archipelago home to some of Africa's most exquisite beaches.

Famous for its snow-white sand spits that peek through aqua blue waters with each outgoing tide, and home to myriad wildlife including pink flamingos, turtles and more than 200 species of fish, this five-island archipelago just off mainland Mozambique has been described by the World Wildlife Fund as a 'Gift to the Earth'.

The exclusivity of the Bazaruto, designated a national park in 1971, is part of the appeal for deep-pocketed visitors – there are hotels on only two of the islands (Bazaruto and Benguera), and they're all high-end. But travellers on a budget can still have the chance to laze on its untouched beaches, snorkel atop offshore reefs and visit wildlife habitats on day tours by dhow (traditional sailing boat) and motorboat operated from the mainland town of Vilankulo. With a good chance of spotting dolphins and even dugongs from the boat, it's an African safari of another kind.

Country Mozambique • **Region** Bazaruto National Park • **Type** beaches • **Cost** cost of day trip or hotel • **Family friendly** not really • **Activities** snorkelling, scuba diving

Look out for dolphins ~
Swim with colourful fish ~
Take a trip on a dhow ~
Powder-soft sands

How do I get here?
There are small airports on Bazaruto and Benguera islands but most visitors fly into Vilankulo on the coast of Mozambique and take a helicopter or boat transfer to their island hotel.

What are the accommodation options like in Vilankulo?
There are sleeping options to suit every budget in this southern Mozambique travel hub, and some decent beaches, too.

How far away is Tofo?
Mozambique's best-known beach town, famous for its whale sharks and manta rays, lies 315km (196 miles) to the south. But the beaches are better in the Bazaruto.

When is the best time to go?
Aim for the May-to-November dry season.

Inspirational Islands

It's rumoured that Bob Dylan's 1976 single 'Mozambique' was inspired by his stay at the Hotel Santa Carolina on Santa Carolina island (then known as Paradise Island), which was abandoned in 1973. The ruins are still visible today.

DEVIL'S POOL

Witness the might and power of Victoria Falls with a spine-tingling dip in the world's most thrilling infinity pool perched atop the falls.

One of Africa's biggest tourist attractions, Victoria Falls ticks a lot of 'must-see-before-you-die' boxes – not only is it the world's largest waterfall, it's one of the Seven Natural Wonders of the World and a Unesco World Heritage Site. There are many vantage points to take in the spectacular views of this majestic beauty, but none quite compare to those from Devil's Pool.

Known locally as *Mosi-oa-Tunya* (the smoke that thunders), the falls drop up to one million litres (264,172 gallons) of water per second into the Zambezi Gorge. A trip out to Livingstone Island to Devil's Pool gets you up close to the power of this natural wonder. Daredevils leap into this natural infinity pool, set at the top of the falls, to peer down at the incredible 108m (354ft) drop. With the roar coming from the curtain of water and the clouds of mist the force of its plunge creates, it's not hard to tell why it got its name 'the smoke that thunders'.

Country Zambia • **Town** Livingstone • **Type** natural pool • **Cost** tours start at US$105 • **Family friendly:** no

Take a dip and peer down the curtain of water from the top of the falls. Not for the faint-hearted!

How can I reach Devil's Pool?

The pool can only be visited on a tour. Tours run from the town of Livingstone where a boat takes you to the island and from there it's a short rocky walk and swim to the pool.

Sounds pretty dangerous, is it?

It's certainly pretty scary and not without its risks. The only thing separating the pool from the drop is a rock lip (known as the Devil's Armchair) that protrudes upwards creating a small barrier. Always follow your guide's instructions.

Is it accessible all year-round?

Nope, it's only possible to swim in the pool in the drier months between mid-August and mid-January.

What exactly is the pool?

Years of rock erosion have created a number of small natural pools at the top of the falls. Devil's Pool is one of these that sits right at the edge of the falls.

Can my kids swim in the pool too?

Only children 12 years old and over are permitted to swim.

Extra Adrenaline Kicks

If a leap into Devil's Pool has you raring for more adventure, you'll find plenty of action around the falls. Take the 111m (364ft) leap on a bungee jump from the Victoria Falls bridge into the Zambezi River, or get wet on a white-water rafting trip down the river with Grade 5 rapids.

CAMPS BAY BEACH

Make like a Capetonian and sign up for a day of fun in the sun at the city's most famous beach.

South Africa isn't short of beautiful beaches, but with its soft white sand, azure water and a backdrop of the spectacular Twelve Apostles range (part of Table Mountain), it's difficult to top Camps Bay beach. Sure, it can be windy and gets crowded during the summer months, but people-watching is part of the appeal of Cape Town's most famous patch of sand, which lies in one of the city's poshest neighbourhoods.

At the southern end of the beach you'll find a tidal pool perfect for kids, while the northern end, which merges into Glen Bay beach, beckons surfers. Hugging the coast, Victoria Rd is lined with cafes, bars and restaurants that will tempt you to make a day of it.

Country: South Africa • **City:** Cape Town • **Type** beach • **Cost:** free • **Activities:** boat trip • **Family friendly:** yes

Find your patch of sand at Cape Town's most famous beach

A Blue Flag Beach

Camps Bay beach has been a Blue Flag beach since 2008. This certification by the Denmark-based Foundation for Environmental Education recognises beaches and marinas that maintain high environmental and quality standards.

Can I bring my own drinks?
Only if they're non-alcoholic – booze is banned on Cape Town's beaches.

What's the best beach bar?
On Victoria Rd, Café Caprice is a popular spot to sip an artisan cocktail as the sun goes down, with DJs spinning deep house from Thursday to Sunday.

Is it safe to swim here?
Generally yes, but be mindful that it can get rough. Lifeguards patrol the beach during busy periods.

How far is Camps Bay from the city centre?
About 7km south (4.3 miles), or 10 to 15 minutes in a taxi. You can also get here on the MyCiYi bus network.

Is there a good time to go?
While the water can be calmer in the mornings, the beach's west-facing outlook makes it the perfect sunset spot.

AMERICAS

THE EXUMAS

A string of mostly uninhabited islands are scattered across central Bahamas with pristine beaches, first-rate diving and those famous swimming pigs.

Stretching across the Bahamas, the Exumas – more than 300 islands and cays – are the stuff of pure paradise and are surrounded by colourful coral reefs and glass-clear waters. The main islands, Great Exuma and Little Exuma, are home to knockout beaches and a clutch of excellent resorts and restaurants, while the secluded Exuma Cays are ripe for island hopping. You'll need to either have your own boat or charter one in order to explore this stunning string of islands, some of which are privately owned.

The highlight of the Exuma Cays is the Exuma Cays Land and Sea Park, 283 sq km (109 sq miles) of protected islands, reef, cay and sea. It was founded as the world's first land-and-sea reserve in 1958 and, unsurprisingly, offers world-class diving. But the real stars of the show here are to be found on Big Major Cay (Pig Island) – the swimming pigs of the Bahamas.

Country The Bahamas · **Type** beach, islands · **Activities** swimming with pigs, diving, snorkelling · **Family friendly** yes

How do I get here?
There are flights from Nassau, the capital of the Bahamas, to the Exumas.

Where will I find the best diving?
The diving is incredible here, particularly in the Exuma Cays Land and Sea Park. Serious divers can also head to Staniel Cay to explore the underwater cave system Thunderball Grotto (made famous in the eponymous 1965 Bond film).

Sounds pricey, is there any budget accommodation?
Many of the accommodation options are higher-end resorts. But you will find some cheaper hotels in George Town, the major centre of the Exumas.

Is human interaction harmful to the pigs?
Copycat attractions and unregulated operations have led to concerns from animal rights advocates about the mistreatment of the pigs. If you take a tour, be sure to choose a reputable operator who keeps the boat at a respectful distance. And don't touch, as they can bite.

The quintessential tropical paradise ~ These swine love to splash around ~ A man prepares conch, a Bahamian delicacy

Pigs Might... Swim?

In recent years the swimming pigs of the Bahamas have become a huge tourist attraction, though it's thought these wild pigs may have been stranded on the island (Big Major Cay) for over a decade. They have become skilled swimmers and will swim out to boats in search of food

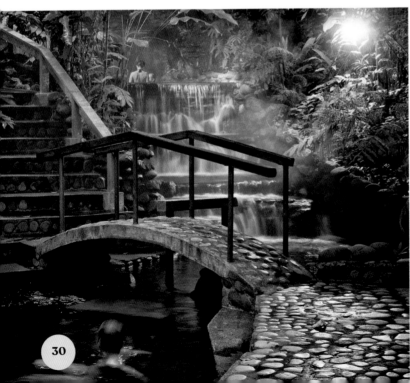

ARENAL HOT SPRINGS

Where there's serious geothermal activity, big things happen. Like volcanoes. And natural hot springs. Arenal is the best of both.

There's a multitude of hot springs in the area surrounding Arenal, Costa Rica's most famous and, until 2010, most active volcano. East of Arenal, however, the village of La Fortuna is especially well known for its concentration of spas that tap into the area's mineral-rich, magma-heated waters.

In keeping with the diverse desires of relaxation-seeking visitors, La Fortuna's thermal springs come in all shapes and sizes. Some keep it natural and showcase their eco-credentials, while others appeal to families with kid-ready extras like water slides. Some are integrated into full-service resorts, whereas others choose to focus only on hot-springs services.

The salutary effects of unwinding in natural warm- and cold-water pools can never be overstated, especially in the magical, jungle-thick environment of which these springs are a part.

Country Costa Rica • **Town** La Fortuna • **Type** hot springs •
Website www.arenal.net/hot-springs • **Cost** varies •
Family friendly some facilities but not others

Arenal volcano, source of the springs ~ Look out for the white-nosed coati ~ Rejuvenate in mineral-rich waters

Is it safe to be so near the volcano?
Nobody knows, but based on Arenal's history, it could be hundreds of years before it erupts again. While it is definitely still active – it vents water vapour, not toxic gases – it hasn't done anything dramatic since 2010 and was inactive for 400 years before its recent 42 years of spectacle.

What's the cost?
It depends. Facilities range from full-scale luxury resorts to much humbler establishments. Around La Fortuna, there's also the river, which runs hot, fast... and free.

Are the waters therapeutic?
The area's waters are rich in minerals like magnesium, sodium, calcium, potassium, carbonates and sulfates. These are said to help alleviate arthritis, cramping, rheumatism, eczema and dermatitis.

What about going with my kids?
Children will enjoy the hot springs at any location, but look for places with affordable day rates and fun extras like water slides. Try to avoid upscale couples' retreats.

How are the Hot Springs Created?

The Arenal volcano was nearly constantly active from 1968 to 2010. What fired its eruptions is also responsible for heating an enormous underground reservoir. This thermal aquifer finds natural and pumped outlets to the surface where it forms hot springs, an abundance of which are scattered around Arenal's base.

QUEEN'S BATHS

Spotting Sea Turtles

Eleuthera is home to a higher concentration of sea turtles than any other Bahamian island. Four of the world's seven species can be found here, especially in the Atlantic-side waters of the island's rural middle and its southern tip. Dive or snorkel to spy them munching on sea grass.

Who needs a Jacuzzi when you could be splashing around in these craggy, sun-warmed natural rock pools overlooking the sea?

It's hard not to dip into tourism-brochure-speak when describing Eleuthera. Shaped like a skinny boomerang, the island has the kind of pink-sand beaches and turquoise waters that just plead for clichés like 'paradise' and 'tropical Eden'. Add in natural rock hot tubs and it's almost impossible not to blurt out 'slice of heaven'.

Scramble up into the cliffs on the island's Atlantic side to find the Queen's Baths, a series of rock pools filled by splashing waves. At low or medium tide you can soak in their shallow, bathtub-warm waters, stretching out and wiggling your toes like you're monarch of the realm. The waves bring in sea creatures too, so don't be surprised to be sharing your tub with a handful of excited minnows or a few drowsy sea snails. When high tide rolls in the baths are too wave-slammed for safe soaking.

Country The Bahamas · **Region** Eleuthera · **Type** natural pools · **Family friendly** yes

Slide in for a soak in Eleuthera's stunning natural rock pools

THE JOY OF WATER

Where on the island are the Queen's Baths?
Near the northern end, where the island gets so thin it seems like it's pinched by a giant's hand. Park on the east side of the Queen's Highway and look for the marker.

Is there anything to see nearby?
The Glass Window Bridge is Eleuthera's most Instagrammable spot. The island gets so skinny here you can look down and see the Caribbean Sea on the left and the Atlantic Ocean on the right.

What if I get hungry? Where can I sleep?
Head up to Harbour Island (though call it 'Briland' if you want to sound local). It seems laid-back, but it's actually huge with celebrities. They come here when they want to eat cheeseburgers barefoot and lay on the pink sand without a swarm of paparazzi.

Anything else to know?
Wear shoes! The rocks can be sharp, and nothing ruins a nice saltwater soak like a stinging cut.

LENÇÓIS MARANHENSES

Desperate with thirst, those lost in the desert might believe they see water when it's only a mirage. But these sand dune pools are delightfully real.

Stretching 1550 sq km (598 sq miles) along Brazil's northeastern coast, the fittingly named Lençóis Maranhenses (bed sheets of Maranhão) is a vast national park of gentle powder-white dunes filled with crystal-clear rainwater lagoons. Taking a dip here is a singular experience. Floating on your back, the only sound you'll hear is that of tiny bubbles popping by your fingertips and the only thing moving will be the clouds above.

Lençóis Maranhenses is often mistakenly referred to as a desert, but it gets too much rain to fit that definition. Instead, two rivers push sand to the Atlantic Ocean and intense winds send it 50km (31 miles) inland. When the sand mixes with mud beneath mangrove trees, it turns the once-lush forest into dust. Each year, more and more forest – and even entire villages – are swallowed up by the majestic, yet menacing sand. It is breathtaking to see the creeping change year over year.

Country Brazil · **Region** Maranhão · **Type** lagoon · **Activities** kayaking, windsurfing · **Family friendly** yes

Slide down for a lagoon splash ~Sink your toes into silky sand ~ Get an aerial view on a plane ride

Are there really no crowds?

OK sure, there are tours near the town of Barreirinhas, particularly from July to September when the lagoons are at their deepest. But if you enter from Santo Amaro or visit Atins, a windsurfing village, solitude is truly possible.

What's the best way to see it?

From the tiny airport in Barreirinhas, fly over in a vintage plane: the rolling sheets from this vantage point are incredible. Most people lagoon hop on 4WD tours. The really adventurous wake up before the sun blazes and do multi-day treks along the dunes to the village oases Queimada dos Britos and Baixa Grande.

Is there any wildlife?

Rivers contain wolffish and locals sometimes add fish to the lagoons. On the dunes, villagers graze cattle and goats, ever wary of the vultures that soar overhead. Though rare, you may see yellow armadillos, white-eared possums or Brazilian slider turtles; the latter tend to wash up on shore, tragically killed by shrimper fishing nets.

"The dunes are moving *very* quickly, which is worrying the families that live there. From August on we have very strong winds, which cover houses in sand including my uncles' who live in one of the oases. They already moved twice in three decades."

Charles Santo Silva of Santo Amaro, local guide

SEMUC CHAMPEY

Bathe, soak up some sunshine or marvel at the geological wonder that created this system of azure swimming pools suspended above a rushing river.

The name Semuc Champey literally means 'where the water rushes beneath the stones' and it couldn't be more accurate – or the place more amazing: in a narrow chasm lies a series of natural swimming pools carved by currents into a limestone bridge above a river. Dubbed by many as the most beautiful place in all of Guatemala, Semuc Champey is an idyllic, otherworldly spot to swim, laze, enjoy the scenery and marvel at the natural world.

Bring your bathing suit and a towel, and prepare for a relaxed and lazy afternoon. If you get tired of swimming you can try a rope swing, hike to a viewpoint or clamber down to the river below. Though increasingly touristed, it's still possible to have a pool or two all to yourself – especially if you overnight and arrive early in the morning – sharing it with a kingfisher or a shy agouti or two.

Country Guatemala • **Region** Lanquín • **Type** natural pool • **Cost** Q50 • **Activities** wild swimming, rope swinging • **Family friendly** yes

How do I get here?
Getting here is a lot of fun, requiring a bumpy, bouncy ride in a 4WD through thick jungle and down steep, unmaintained roads. Just as you're wondering if you'll ever reach it, you spot it far below you: a ladder-like series of squarish azure holes visible through the lush vegetation.

How big are these pools?
Some are big, easily as large as a community swimming pool. Others are more like a hotel's indoor pool.

Can I come with my family?
Yes! In fact, it's easy to see everyone from Grandma and Grandpa to a bunch of toddlers in water wings heading down the path for a fun day spent swimming.

Can you tell me a bit about the location?
On either side, the valley walls rise up steeply, giving a Shangri-La sense of this being a world forgotten...though the girls selling chocolates (some can sell them to you in eight different languages!) will remind you that reality isn't far away.

The approach by wooden bridge to Semuc Champey ~ Lie back and relax ~ Take in the scenery from your pool

Take Care

Tour guides may offer the chance to clamber down to the rushing river beneath the pools – it's geologically fascinating and well worth a peek, but be careful! The current is strong, the rocks can be slippery, and if you get injured you are hours away from the nearest medical care.

BLUE LAGOON

Take a dip in the stunning Caribbean lagoon that launched Brooke Shields' career.

Surrounded by lush, green jungle on three sides and meeting the ocean on the other, the dazzling aquamarine lagoon named for the 1980 Hollywood film shot largely in Jamaica is one of the most beautiful spots in the country. About 20 minutes' drive east of Port Antonio on the nation's northeast coast, the 55m- (180ft-) wide lagoon gets its incredible hue from freshwater springs that mix with the warm Caribbean Sea. Should you decide to take a dip (and you should), you'll notice the peculiar sensation of the temperate alternating between tropical to downright frosty as you paddle around.

At the entry to the lagoon, you're bound to encounter local operators eager to take you on a short boat ride (US$30) to nearby Cocktail Beach (where parts of the Tom Cruise movie *Cocktail* were filmed) and rustic Monkey Island, a short distance away, but playing around on the rope swing is just as fun.

Country Jamaica · **Region** Portland Parish · **Type** lagoon · **Activities** boat and paddle-raft tours · **Family friendly:** yes

Boats wait at the lagoon entrance to ferry visitors over to nearby Cocktail Beach

© Westend61 | Getty Images

I heard the water changes colour. True or false?
True! Due to the mixing of fresh water and seawater, the lagoon sometimes takes on a turquoise hue, while at other times it turns a deep indigo blue. If it has been raining heavily, runoff water from the hills turns the lagoon a disappointing murky green.

Is there a beach here?
Only a small, unmemorable one – this is more of a place you come to for a quick swim or a raft tour rather than to spend the whole day. Note that the area is currently under development so there may be more facilities (and maybe an entry fee) here at some point.

Can I stay on the lagoon?
Yes! The charming Kanopi House has direct access to the lagoon, and there are plenty of other hotels in the area.

On Location

It's commonly thought that *The Blue Lagoon* was filmed here, but while some scenes from the controversial flick (which sees two shipwrecked cousins forge a sexual relationship) were shot in Jamaica, the lagoon scenes were actually filmed in a Mediterranean lagoon that lies between the Maltese island of Comino and the islet of Cominotto.

MOOSEHEAD LAKE

There's something elemental about the lakes of Maine: fresh air and pure water hemmed in by green hills. Natural solace for body and soul.

The Maine Highlands are full of glorious lakes, but evocatively named Moosehead Lake, 160km (99 miles) north of Augusta, is the largest and arguably most sublime. (It's also the largest lake in the eastern United States.) While there's joy in spying at it from the surrounding hills, especially the heights of Mt Kineo, rising 545m (1788ft) above its shore, nothing delivers Moosehead's healthy, natural and peaceful punch like getting right in its waters.

A leisurely canoe along Moosehead's shoreline takes in sweeping vistas and encourages snooping on the wildlife (perhaps even a moose!), most rewardingly in the extensive lands – more than a third of the area around the lake – set aside for protection and conservation.

One heads-up: given Moosehead Lake's dimensions – 190km by 64km (118 miles by 40 miles) – it has a long fetch, which can make for choppy water in strong winds. It's best to save stand-up paddleboarding for balmier days.

Country USA • **Region** Maine Highlands • **Type** lake • **Activities** SUP, canoeing, wild swimming • **Family friendly**: yes

© Catherine Ledner | Getty Images

Moose-Watching

Along the lake shorefront, stay alert for local fauna such as ruffed grouse, rabbits, wild turkeys, deer, bears and of course moose. For moose, which outnumber people in the region three to one, May and June are best for sightings, as are dawn and dusk in shady wetlands like marshes and bogs.

Get into the swing of things at the largest lake in the eastern USA

At what time of year is the water best?
From Memorial Day (25 May) to September is typically prime season for boating, when the water levels are high. Regardless of the time of the year, care should always be taken in shallow coves.

How can I reach the water?
There are public launches in Greenville, Rockwood and Seboomook. Campgrounds and local operators also usually offer water access.

Do I have to bring my own gear?
No, paddleboards, canoes and life vests can be rented from local shops and outfitters, some of which also provide pickup and delivery services to launch points.

Are there any special rules about swimming?
Not as such, but caution is important, especially in areas with boat traffic and once water levels drop enough that normally submerged obstacles become hazards. Notably, even by August the water will still be cold but not uncomfortable.

DOS OJOS CENOTE

Take a refreshing dip – or maybe a cave dive – in a natural waterhole that connected ancient Mayans to another realm.

Cenotes were a major part of ancient Mayan life for both practical and spiritual reasons. With few rivers and lakes in the Yucatán region, these natural wells created by the collapse of the limestone bedrock, exposing subterranean waterbodies underneath, were a primary water source. But the Mayans also believed that cenotes were a portal to speak with the gods, and used them for sacrificial offerings.

Swimming in these crystal-clear turquoise pools today, it's easy to understand why they held the Mayans in awe. Named for the eye-like appearance of two neighbouring cenotes from above, Dos Ojos is widely considered to be the most beautiful cenote in the Tulum area. The entrance ticket allows you to swim in the main cenote and part of the second, but you'll need to book a snorkelling tour to visit the rest of the site, including a cave full of bats.

Country Mexico · **Region** Yucatán Peninsula · **Type** natural pool · **Cost** M$350 · **Activities** scuba diving · **Family friendly** yes

Is the water cold?
At 25°C (77°F), the water in Dos Ojos isn't much cooler than the Caribbean Sea.

What's the best time to visit?
Aim to get here before 9am to avoid the crowds. The cenote is open from 8am to 5pm.

Is there any marine life in the cenote?
The water is so clear you may spot tiny freshwater fish even without a snorkel. Two species of freshwater shrimp also call the cenote home.

Are there any facilities at the cenote?
The cenote is well developed for tourism but fortunately the infrastructure doesn't detract from its natural beauty. You can rent snorkels and book with a tour company in Tulum for scuba diving.

Haven't I seen this place on TV?
Probably. Dos Ojos has been featured in a handful of films and documentaries, including the 2006 BBC series *Planet Earth*.

Book a diving tour to explore the underwater cave ~ Join the crowd splashing about in one of Tulum's most beautiful cenotes ~ The natural beauty of Dos Ojos, which featured in the BBC's *Planet Earth*

Dos Ojos meets Sac Actun

In 2018, a connection was found between Dos Ojos and a nearby cave system, Sac Actun (p66). The smaller Dos Ojos became a part of Sac Actun, making Sac Actun the longest known underwater cave system in the world.

HAMILTON POOL PRESERVE

An idyllic waterfall-fed pool at the heart of a nature preserve, Hamilton Pool is one of the best excursions in day-trip distance of Austin, Texas.

Nothing is as iconic of a Central Texas summer as a swimming hole, and for Austinites the be-all-and-end-all of swimming holes is Hamilton Pool. Fed by a 15.2m- (50ft-) high waterfall, the cool, jade-coloured water tempts locals to exchange the oppressive Texan heat for a hidden oasis less than an hour from the city. Formed by an underground stream known today as Hamilton Creek, the limestone roof here collapsed thousands of years ago, leaving in its place a pool half-shaded by the remnants of the natural dome and surrounded by chunks of limestone, perfect as platforms for soaking up the sun.

While the waterfall's flow fluctuates depending on the season, the pool's level remains nearly constant (though it does close during heavy rains). The steep and rocky path down to the water passes through a short stretch of forest before turning the final corner to the first incredible view of the pool.

Country USA · **City** Austin, Texas · **Type** natural pool · **Cost** US$26 per vehicle · **Activities** swimming, light hiking · **Family friendly** yes

Cool off on a hot Texas summer day at this tucked-away oasis

Reservations

As one of Austin's favourite swimming holes, Hamilton Pool has established daily limits on visitor numbers, and they often book up a month or more in advance during the summer. Reservations are split into morning and afternoon sessions – show up for the correct time or you'll be denied entry.

Y'all got reservations for Hamilton Pool? Very lucky to land those on such short notice!

I know, we're excited! Any tips on packing?
Well, there's nothing here except life jackets for visitors. Take your towels, sunscreen, food, water – really anything you need for the day.

And a couple of cold brews for the afternoon?!
You do know it's alcohol-free? That's probably the quickest way to get kicked out.

Is there anything else to do nearby after we leave?
Milton Reimers Ranch Park is 1.5km (1 mile) down the road. It's more well known among Austin's trail-biking and rock-climbing communities, but there's a really nice stretch of the Pedernales River that's also good for swimming when Hamilton Pool is full. Even better, both sites are on the same entrance ticket so they're perfect to combine into one long day.

CRATER LAKE NATIONAL PARK

Framed by a forest-clad volcanic crater, the water of this lake is so pure and deep that it resembles a blue mirror.

Gazing from the rim of this 1883m- (6178ft-) high crater into the deepest lake in the USA is worth every effort to get here. The water's enchanting indigo tones reflect the surrounding evergreen-covered cliffs and fast-moving clouds high in the sky. Snow covers the ground much of the year and adds bright white sparkle.

Some people do nothing more at Crater Lake than unfold a travel chair at a viewpoint and gaze, sometimes for hours, at the hypnotising beauty. Driving, snow shoeing, taking a trolley tour or cross-country skiing the 53km (33 mile) rim will give you more variety of sublime angles to ooh and ah at. But it's getting on the lake via official boat tour (no other watercraft are allowed) or swimming in the clear, cold water, that offer a near-spiritual experience. Float on your back to marvel at the high edges of the crater and daydream about lava and ice.

Country USA · **Region** Oregon · **Type** lake · **Cost** parking pass US$15-25 · **Activities** wild swimming, biking, fishing, snow shoeing, hiking, boat tours · **Family friendly** yes

© Melissa Shosey | Shutterstock. © Kris Wiktor | Shutterstock. © massimo colombo | Getty Images (following page)

Take the plunge into the deepest lake in the US ~ Hike to a viewpoint overlooking the glassy water

Is the lake really in the crater of a volcano?

Yes! Around 7,700 years ago, Mt Mazama experienced an eruption so massive that ash particles have been found as far away as Greenland. Crater Lake is in the collapsed caldera and while the volcano's most violent days are over, it's still active.

Does the snow ever melt? Does the lake ever freeze?

Despite the fact that snowfall averages 13m (43ft) per year, the last time the lake completely froze was 1949. Usually most of the snow melts by August, and snowfall begins again around October, but some years the snow never fully melts. This means chilly water temperatures that max out at around 16°C (61°F).

Why is it so blue?

That's pure snowmelt! And it's 592m (1942ft) deep. Unlike most lakes, there are no streams that flow in or out. Water molecules reflect only the color blue so when there are no interfering sediments, pollution or algae, only the blue shines through.

Go Fish

No fish lived in Crater Lake until it was stocked with five species by humans between the years 1888 and 1941. Today only kokanee salmon and rainbow trout have survived. You can try your luck fishing for them from Wizard Island in the middle of the lake, no permit required.

HAVASU FALLS

Aquamarine waters gush over burnt-orange cliffs into vibrant-blue pools surrounded by spiritual desert at Havasupai Reservation.

One of the Grand Canyon's most impressive natural treasures, Havasu Falls is actually a series of five spring-fed waterfalls hidden away in a valley within the 74,867-hectare (185,000-acre) Havasupai Reservation and reached by a 12-to-16km (8-to-10 mile) hike. These stunning blue-green waterfalls plunging into sparkling blue pools below get their hue from parts of the canyon floor and rocks underneath the falls that are made up of limestone deposited by the flowing water.

At the main Havasu Falls, the waterfall drops 30m (100ft) into the brilliant-blue pool, making it a popular swimming spot. The largest of the falls is Mooney Falls; its water gushes down from a height of 60m (200ft), but it sees fewer visitors due to the difficulty in reaching it. You need to climb through a couple of tunnels and hike a very steep trail – not for the faint-hearted. Most people take the easier trail to admire the view from the top instead.

Country USA · **Region** Arizona · **Type** waterfall · **Cost** US$100-125 for permit · **Activities** hiking, swimming · **Family friendly** no

It's a hike to get here but well worth the effort

Sounds incredible, how can I visit?
To maintain the pristine beauty and protect the environment, visitor numbers are limited. There is no day hiking permitted in the canyon; you must have reservations at Havasupai Lodge or for camping and entrance fees need to be paid in advance.

When is the best time to visit the falls?
Peak season is May to September when water temperatures average around 15 to 21°C (60 to 70°F).

What supplies do I need to take?
Pack all of your food before the hike in case the cafes in town are not open. It's recommended that each person carry a minimum of 3.5L (1 gallon) of water to keep hydrated. And take all of your rubbish with you when you leave.

And I can just get one of the pack mules to carry my stuff?
There are ongoing allegations of animal cruelty, abuse and overpacking of the mules. Avoid using them, pack light and carry your own gear.

The People of the Blue-Green Waters

The Havasupai Tribe has a long connection to the land of the Havasupai Reservation and it is the only Native American tribe that lives below the rim in the Grand Canyon today. They call themselves the Havasu Baaja, the People of the Blue-Green Waters. Keep in mind that it's a privilege to visit their sacred land.

LAKE POWELL

In the vast desert of the Southwest, this ribbon of sandstone and sun brings families and modern-day explorers into a labyrinthine water wonderworld.

Lake Powell sits in one of the most desolate corners of the US Southwest. Here among sandstone cathedrals along the profound waters of the dammed Colorado River, you will find peace, serenity and a unique connection with a vast network of canyons, natural amphitheatres, cliffside archaeological sites and more.

This is the second-biggest man-made reservoir in the United States. The sheer size of the flooded paradise is truly impressive. The reservoir stretches for 300km (186 miles) across the states of Arizona and Utah, and has close to 3220km (2000 miles) of shoreline.

You can experience all of it aboard a houseboat, speedboat or even canoe, exploring narrow passageways of the flooded Glen Canyon. There are natural bridges to be visited, ruins from Ancestral Puebloan civilisations, side hikes, swimming and waterskiing, and enough adventures to fill a full week with family or friends.

Country USA · **Region** Utah and Arizona · **Type** lake · **Cost** national park entrance US$30 · **Activities** houseboating, waterskiing, SUP, canoeing · **Family friendly** yes

© Gleb Tarro | Shutterstock

Find peace and calm as you float on the water in the tranquil setting of this vast reservoir

Archaeological Finds

The Glenn Canyon Project was one of the largest archaeological digs ever in the US. From 1957 to 1963 an army of scientists, volunteers and even grave robbers raced against time – and the rising tides – to document and preserve the archaeological sites dating back some 12,000 years found in the vast canyon complex.

What type of activities are available?
Most people go out on a houseboat for a week and explore the canyons. If you rent a speedboat, you can take advantage of some killer wakeboarding and waterskiing. On land there are often little side hikes to check out. But it's really the adventures on the water that makes this place special. You could spend a full day just floating on an inner tube or exploring back canyons by stand-up paddleboard.

How's the weather?
This is the middle of the desert, so it's hot and dry in the summer, while nights can get kind of chilly, especially in the early spring and autumn. Skip winter vacations (too cold), if you really want to experience the water.

How's the water?
The waters of Lake Powell are nothing short of spectacular. As water settles and seeps into the sandstone (not good for the environment, but good for aesthetics), it becomes much clearer and translucent. You can even scuba dive here.

SAC ACTUN

Bobbing through just a few hundred metres of the world's longest underwater cave system confirms that the planet is full of hidden wonders.

In January 2018, Sac Actun, which means 'White Cave' in Yucatec Maya, was identified as the longest submerged cave system on the planet – 346km (215 miles) of underground, water-logged labyrinth northeast of Tulum. Fortunately for soft adventurers, there's easy access to a small piece of it that can be appreciated without cave diving equipment or expertise beyond a life vest, a mask and snorkel, comfort in water and a guide.

The approach from ground level is down a steep flight of steps and into the heart of a high-walled cenote. From there, the time in the water is an eerie and magical experience, spent floating effortlessly and slowly into and then through a series of partially flooded, stalagmite- and stalactite-filled caverns, some quite large. Most are gently lit for extra effect, but there's no dampening the sense of having stepped into another world, just as the Mayans thought they had.

Country Mexico · **Region** Riviera Maya · **Type** natural pool · **Website** www.cenotessacactun.com · **Cost** US$40 per person · **Family friendly** yes

Is the water cold?
It's pretty chilly, but not outrageously so. Since the snorkelling doesn't involve vigorous, body-warming swimming, it could help to bring a wetsuit.

Is it really safe?
Yes, if you are at ease in dark, enclosed spaces and able to withstand the water temperature, as most of the 45-minute guided passage is spent floating in deep pools.

Has anything interesting been discovered here?
Absolutely. Sac Actun has been called the most important submerged archaeological site in the world. In addition to numerous pre-Hispanic sites and the remains of extinct plant and animal species, including a mastodon, divers also found what may be the oldest human skeleton unearthed in the New World.

Are pictures permitted?
Yes, although all equipment must be completely waterproof.

Gently float your way through the magical caves.
~ Explore the longest submerged cave system on the planet

What's a Cenote?

Once sacred to the ancient Mayans, cenotes are sinkholes formed by collapsed water-filled caverns. The ground of the Yucatán Peninsula is porous coral limestone, which has been especially susceptible to millennia of changing water levels and erosion. The result: cenotes and the extensive underground river systems that connect them.

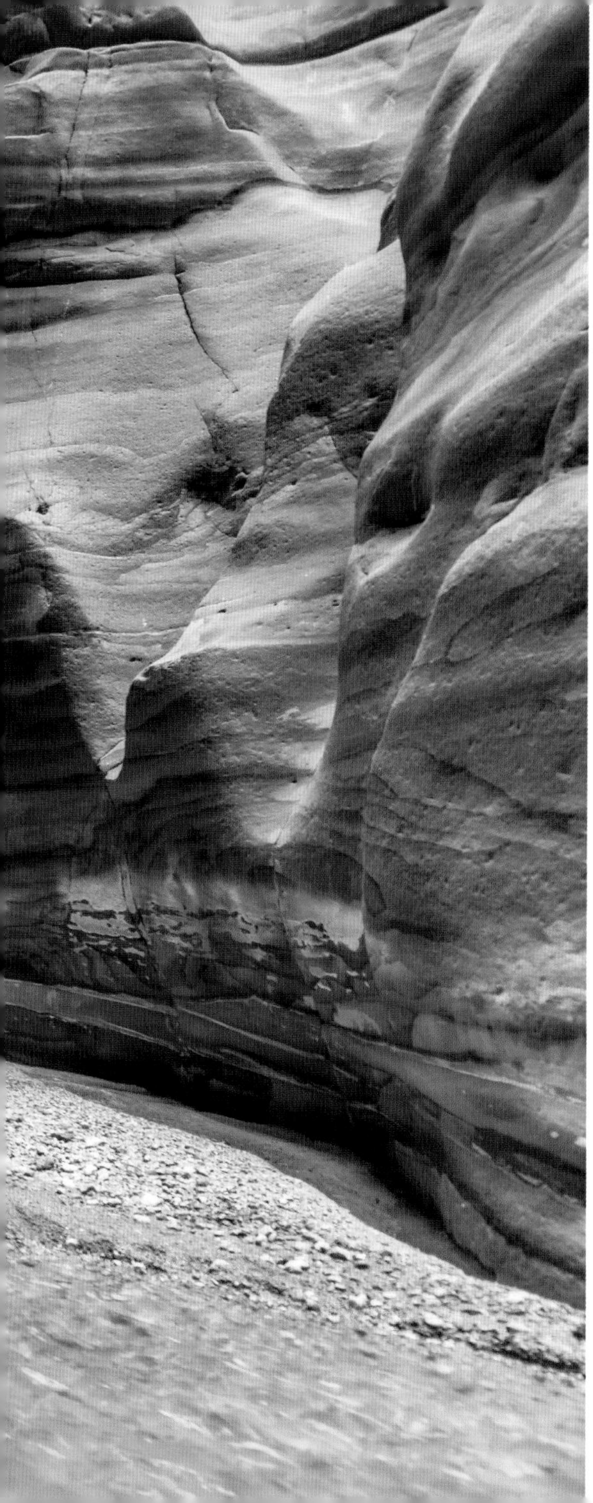

© BargotiPhotography | Getty Images

ASIA

DEAD SEA

Famously the most effortless place to float anywhere in the world, it's all sun, sand, salt and mud on the Dead Sea's shores.

Float effortlessly atop the still sea, with only the sound of water gently lapping against the salt-rock shore. The Dead Sea is not your average swimming spot, and this is not your average day at the beach.

Start with a generous lathering of Dead Sea mud – the thick, dark goo pulled straight from the shoreline is rich in mineral content and is world-renowned for its cosmetic benefits. Pile it on, give it time to dry and crack, and then prepare for a dip in the water to wash it off.

Ease yourself into the deep – the last thing you want to do is splash the salty water into your eyes – until your chest is submerged, then lay gently back until you're staring up at the sky. The classic Dead Sea gag is to sit back in the water and read the day's newspaper, but you won't want to linger too long; many bathers feel itchy after ten minutes in the mineral-rich water.

Country Jordan · **Region** Dead Sea Highway · **Type** salt lake · **Family friendly** yes

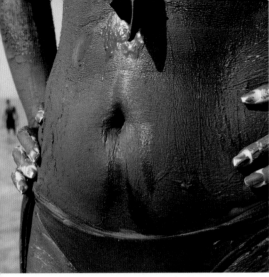

It buuuurns! Why does it burn?
Are you ok? That's all the salt. I guess I should have mentioned that.

Why is there so much salt?
It's mostly from the mountains around here. There's so little vegetation in the desert that when it does rain it almost all runs straight into the sea, carrying the mineral-heavy soil with it.

But isn't that true of lakes all over the world?
Yes, but the Dead Sea has no outlets – water comes in, but has nowhere to go so it just evaporates, leaving the salt behind.

Why is it called the Dead Sea?
It's just too salty to sustain most life – something like ten times the saltiness of the ocean. Scientists have actually found microbes living at the mouths of freshwater springs deep underwater, but the chances of seeing anything while swimming is nil.

Hike to hidden oases ~
Slather yourself in mineral-rich mud ~
Salt-covered shores ~
Kick back and relax

73

Hiking Wadi Arabia

While it's the seashore that gets all the headlines, the stream-fed *wadi* (valley) canyons that surround the Dead Sea in Wadi Arabia are excellent for hiking; from hidden palm-tree oases to towering waterfalls, there are plenty of options for an active adventure to accompany your Dead Sea float.

BEPPU

Bathing opportunities bubble up from underneath the ground all over the town of Beppu, one of Japan's best-known *onsen* (hot-spring) hotspots.

In a country overflowing with hot-spring towns, Beppu is arguably one of the most famous. Located on the island of Kyūshū, the city has eight distinct *onsen* areas offering plentiful opportunities to take a soak in the geothermally heated waters, ranging from pleasantly warm to near scalding in temperature, along with mud baths and seaside *rotemburo* (open-air baths). Together these baths produce more hot-spring water than any other *onsen* resort in the country – around 100 million litres (26 million gallons) of water per day.

Don't miss taking a dip in the steaming hot waters of the Meiji-era Takegawara Onsen, set in a beautiful old wooden building. Afterwards, experience the feeling of being buried alive (up to your neck, at least) in the sand baths (a *yukata*, light cotton kimono, is provided) – the sand is heated by thermal springs and is said to relieve muscle aches.

Country Japan · **Region** Kyūshū · **Type** hot-spring town · **Cost** ¥100–¥1000 · **Family friendly** some facilities but not others

Can I wear bathers in the *onsen*?
Sorry, no. You'll need to strip off before entering the baths, which are sex segregated.

Do I need to bring anything with me?
It's a good idea to bring a towel and soap. A lot of places rent them out but you'll find a few that don't.

So just how hot does the water get at Takegawara?
Too hot for some! It ranges from 43 to 45°C (109 to 113°F).

Is there much else to do in Beppu besides bathing?
The region is known for its abundant bamboo and a visit to the Beppu Traditional Bamboo Crafts Centre is worthwhile to see the collection of elegant bamboo works by Edo-period masters.

What about somewhere to eat and drink?
Beppu is quite a buzzing city with some great eating options and a lively after-dark scene with plenty of bars. The city is particularly known for a few delicacies including *fugu* (puffer fish) and *toriten* (chicken tempura).

Steam rises up all over the city ~ Brave a hot sand bath ~ Boil yourself an *onsen* egg

The Hells

The most famous attraction in Beppu is the very kitsch and touristy *jigoku meguri* (hell circuit). This collection of boiling hot springs is purely for looking at, not for bathing, and you'll see steaming vivid blue and blood-orange waters, while one of the bubbling mud hells is said to resemble a monk's shaved head!

RADHANAGAR BEACH

Seek out some of India's most pristine, sun-dappled sands and thrilling diving on Havelock Island, queen of the distant, mystery-rich Andaman Islands.

Clinging to the northwest coast of seductive jungle-wreathed Havelock Island (the most developed of the far-flung Andaman Islands), showstopping Radhanagar is undeniably one of Asia's most exquisite beaches. Gazing out on this glorious white-gold stretch of silken sand washed by turquoise waves and bordered by tangles of near-impenetrable primeval tropical forest, you could almost be somewhere along Thailand's sugary coastline. In fact, here you're much closer to Southeast Asia than mainland India – which lies over 1300km (808 miles) west!

Havelock tempts travellers with its terrific diving and outstanding local dive schools, but you can also get a taste of the island's underwater riches with just a leisurely spot of snorkelling off Radhanagar. Otherwise, there's little to do here apart from stroll the beach's vast expanses and kick back on the sand as the sun sinks into the Andaman Sea – and that, of course, is what it's all about.

Country India · **Region** Andaman Islands · **Type** beach · **Activities** swimming, snorkelling, diving · **Family friendly** yes

Scuba dive, splash about or just sunbathe on one of India's most spectacular beaches

THE JOY OF WATER

What's the snorkelling and diving like?
Havelock's glass-clear waters are famous for their dazzling rainbows of fish, while deep-sea corals await divers venturing beyond the shallows. You might even spot a shark, turtle or manta ray.

When is the best time to visit?
Radhanagar's fiery sunsets are outrageously popular, but if you swing by early in the day you'll have much of the beach to yourself. December to March are the top months for diving, snorkelling and beaching about.

Where can I eat and sleep?
A large part of Radhanagar's allure is its lack of development: there are only a couple of luxury resorts here. Pick between the elegantly rustic cottages at island original Barefoot at Havelock, where you can feast on fresh grilled fish at your own private beach table, or the glitzy private-pool villas and sophisticated restaurants shrouded by rainforest at recently opened Taj Exotica.

Croc Warning

Crocodiles are a serious danger in the Andaman Islands and there have been several fatal attacks on tourists in recent years. Make sure you're up to date on the latest safety information, follow any official local warnings and keep out of the water at dusk and dawn.

RAJA AMPAT ISLANDS

With thousands of fish sparkling like spilt glitter and darting around castles of coral, the warm, clear waters of Raja Ampat hide living underwater treasure.

Home to some of the most pristine coral reefs on our watery planet, Raja Ampat has fast swum into the international diving consciousness. Here divers (and snorkellers) splash about among overwhelming shoals of sardines, bubble over walking sharks, are charmed by the whirls of colourful nudibranchs, cower in fear during shark feeding frenzies and smile at comical turtles and soaring manta rays. With so much going for it, it's not surprising that many experienced divers consider Raja Ampat the planet's best dive destination.

The attractions of Raja Ampat don't stop at the high-tide line. With hundreds of jagged, jungle-covered islands and bizarre mushroom-shaped islets, ringed by dazzling white-sand beaches that pop up out of placid turquoise waters, this is also fantasy island-hopping terrain. And what better way to enjoy it than by paddling a kayak between islands or sailing on a luxury live-aboard boat?

Country Indonesia · **Region** West Papua (island of Papua) · **Type** archipelago · **Activities** scuba diving, snorkelling, kayaking, island hopping· **Family friendly** yes

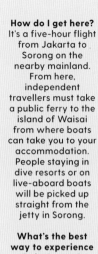

Dolphins frolic between the islands ~ Fish are camouflaged in the colourful reef ~ Possibly the world's best diving destination ~ Just paddling about

How do I get here?
It's a five-hour flight from Jakarta to Sorong on the nearby mainland. From here, independent travellers must take a public ferry to the island of Waisai from where boats can take you to your accommodation. People staying in dive resorts or on live-aboard boats will be picked up straight from the jetty in Sorong.

What's the best way to experience Raja Ampat?
Dedicated divers will want to organise everything through one of the luxury dive lodges, while those just here to enjoy some snorkelling and the sheer beauty of the place can chill out in one of the homestays found on some islands. For the ultimate Raja Ampat experience though, sail into the sunset on a luxury live-aboard boat.

Is the diving suitable for beginners?
In a word – no. Most dive sites have strong currents and are drift dives. This isn't really the place to come to get your first taste of diving. However, the snorkelling is unsurpassed.

Where Coral Reefs Are Born

Scientists believe that due to the sheer number and variety of fish and corals in the waters surrounding the Raja Ampat Islands the archipelago acts as a nursery ground, which restocks coral reefs across the South Pacific and eastern Indian Ocean.

RIVER GANGES, RISHIKESH

Swimming is part purification, part prayer at Rishikesh, where the sacred River Ganges bursts out of the Himalaya and enters the plains.

Devout Hindus believe that the Ganges has the power to wash away sins, and it certainly feels that way if you plunge into the ice-cold waters of the sacred river at Rishikesh. While nearby Haridwar is the precise spot where Hindus declare that the Ganges has left the mountains for the plains, swimming upriver at Rishikesh feels spiritually closer to the Himalaya, and physically further from the polluted megacities of the Indo-Gangetic Plain. At this point, the waters are crystal clear and the river traces a green and winding gorge, lined with temples, yoga ashrams and sacred ghats, and book-ended by sweeping suspension bridges.

Pilgrims mill at the water's edge, but a full immersion involves braving mountain-chilled waters and powerful currents. If you dare to try, grip tightly to the chains set into the riverbanks, or bathe in calmer curves of the river upstream from Lakshman Jhula.

Country India • **Region** Uttarakhand • **Type** river •
Activities wild swimming, yoga, rafting, puja ceremonies •
Family friendly no

Is it safe to swim in the Ganges?
Downstream from Rishikesh, water hygiene would be a serious concern, but there are few major settlements in the mountains to the north, so the waters are icily clear. Currents however are something to take seriously: stay close to the bank and never swim out into the full flow of the river.

What else is there to do in Rishikesh?
Yoga, yoga and more yoga. Rishikesh is India's yoga capital, and dozens of ashrams and yoga centres flank the river offering training for practitioners who are willing to sign up to strict rules on diet and behaviour and a ban on drugs, alcohol and tobacco. For something more recreational, river-rafting trips run from September to November.

When is the best time to visit?
Pilgrims flock to Rishikesh for the holy month of Sawan in July/August, but it's more peaceful to visit from March to June or September to October, avoiding the June-to-August monsoon rains and the chill of deep winter.

Follow in the Beatles' footsteps to this ashram ~ River-rafting on the Ganges ~ Religious offerings adorn the shore ~ Brave the ice-cold waters of the sacred Ganges

Hippy History

Rishikesh marks the spot where Lord Rama did penance after killing the demon king of Lanka, but for Hindus, the focal point of devotion is Haridwar, 20km (12 miles) downstream. It was blissed out hippies who put Rishikesh on the travel map in the 1960s; you can still visit the ruins of the ashram where The Beatles met the Maharishi.

KINOSAKI ONSEN

At this picturesque *onsen* (hot-spring) town a train-ride from Kyoto, take your pick of steaming-hot geothermal waters to soak away your stresses.

Onsen (natural hot-spring baths) bubble up from underground all over Japan and are an integral part of Japanese culture. At Kinosaki, an impossibly pretty, and popular, *onsen* resort town on the Japan Sea coast, you can sample the mineral-rich waters at seven individual public baths spread over the town. The town is a walkable size so it's easy to stroll along its willow-lined canal, hopping between *onsen* as you go. Take a dip in the outdoor cypress-barrel bath at Mandara-yu or feel the welcoming breeze at the rooftop *rotemburo* (open-air bath) at Gosho-no-yu on the main street.

To get the best out of your visit, spend the night in a *ryokan* (traditional lodging) so you can experience the magical lantern-lit evenings, while donning your light, cotton kimono and *geta* (wooden sandals), and clip-clopping through the streets for the ultimate sleep-inducing ritual – a soothing, hot soak.

Country Japan • **Region** Kansai • **Type** hot-spring town •
Cost *yu-meguri* pass (¥1200) gives you entry to all baths •
Family friendly yes

Taste-testing the mineral water ~ *Geta* (traditional wooden sandals) ~ Mineral water for drinking ~ Visitors wear *yukata* (lightweight kimonos) ~ The town is perfect for strolling

What's the best time of year to visit?

Winter (December to February) is the most popular time, when you can escape the chilly temperatures in the piping-hot water. This is high season though, so book ahead.

Can I wear swimwear?

Nope. Naked communal bathing is ingrained in Japanese daily life and no one will bat an eyelid at your nakedness. Wash yourself before you get into the water (watch the Japanese and follow) and once you're in, you'll be so relaxed you'll forget you're nuded up!

I have tattoos, will I be allowed entry?

Yes. Some public bathhouses in Japan do not allow entry to customers with tattoos, but this is not a problem in Kinosaki.

Where should I stay?

Treat yourself to a stay at the historic Nishimuraya Honkan, a beautiful *ryokan* that has been around for 150 years and has its own *onsen* – some rooms even come with private outdoor baths.

Mythical Kinosaki

Kou-no-yu is the oldest *onsen* in Kinosaki at around 1400 years old. Legend has it that it was discovered when a villager spotted an Oriental white stork soaking its injured leg in a pool of water, and soon after it flew off, having been healed.

HAWAIYAT NAJM (BIMMAH SINKHOLE)

Take a refreshing dip in one of Oman's most accessible – and unusual – natural swimming holes.

Sinkholes are often created by groundwater eating away at limestone and carbonate. Caverns form as the minerals dissolve, and eventually the ground above caves in. In Oman's northeast, just off the highway between the villages of Ḏibāb and Bimmah, there's a particularly beautiful example of this natural phenomenon.

Better known as Bimmah Sinkhole, Hawaiyat Najm has a sparkling, semi-circular blue-green pool at its base, its idyllic hue attributed to the mixing of mineral-rich fresh water from underground rivers and the saline water of the ocean just 600m (1968ft) away. A concrete staircase leading down to the pool detracts from the natural beauty of the 50m- (164ft-) wide sinkhole somewhat, but it also makes access a cinch. It's possible to jump into the water from a low cliff on the opposite side of the pool, though the water is not deep enough to safely jump from the top of the sinkhole, which rises 20m (65ft) above the water's surface.

Country Oman · **Region** Muscat Governorate · **Type** natural spring · **Family friendly** yes

Escape the Oman heat with a cool dip in this breathtaking natural phenomenon

How do I get here?
The sinkhole is located about 85 minutes' drive south of Muscat along the main coast road. If you're not keen to hire a car, it's possible to book a tour from the capital.

Is there a good time to come?
Easy accessibility means the sinkhole can get quite busy, especially on weekends, so aim for a weekday in the early morning or late afternoon for more privacy.

Is it OK to wear a bikini?
While it's acceptable to wear a modest bikini at Oman's touristy swimming spots, it's respectful to cover up (a T-shirt and shorts is fine) as soon as you get out of the water.

Is there any marine life in the sinkhole?
Dangle your feet in the pool for a free fish pedicure. If you stand still in the water for a few minutes, the tiny fish will nibble the rest of your body, too.

Is there anything else to do here?
No, making it a great stop on a day trip from Muscat to Wadi Shab.

The Falling Star

The sinkhole's Arabic name translates as 'the falling star'. The name was derived from the long-held view that the sinkhole was created by an ancient meteorite.

SNORKELLING THE SARDINE RUN

With millions of sardines dancing metres from the shoreline, Moalboal's wildlife phenomenon makes for the most enchanting underwater display.

Home to more than 7000 islands, the Philippines boasts bountiful snorkelling sites. The Cebu region in particular is synonymous with marine life and aquatic activities – from swimming with polka-dotted whale sharks to exploring enigmatic wrecks. Nestled in Cebu Island's western shores, Moalboal is home to an almost year-round sardine run.

Snorkelling this paradisiacal haven is ideal for those seeking underwater adventure at a leisurely pace. There's no need to get on a boat or strap on a tank to discover Moalboal's underwater sanctuary. Panagsama Beach's reef is easily accessible due to the sea's calm waters and its proximity to the shoreline. Simply wade into the crystal waters from a blindingly white stretch of sand, dip your head under the surface and find yourself among seemingly infinite masses of sparkling sardines.

Country Philippines • **Region** Moalboal, Cebu Island • **Type** marine reef • **Cost** snorkel hire is available for a minimal fee • **Activities** snorkelling • **Family friendly** yes

What do the shoals look like?
Forego expectations of scaly fish packed tightly into a tin. Instead, picture glimmering figures swirling in synchronised, undulating formations against a deep-blue backdrop, the sunlight glinting on their silvery scales. It's a magically mindful experience.

This sounds pretty special. How can I experience it?
If you don't have your own snorkel gear, you can hire some from beach stores. The sardines themselves can be found at the edge of the drop-off reef. There is a minimal, relaxing current and the tide is calm – just make sure to avoid the rainy season, from June to October. Best of all, development remains relatively slow, so expect to be one of a handful of people in the water.

What else can I expect to see?
If the sardines aren't satiating your deep-sea thrills, the reef wall is a mosaic of hues, adorned with colourful corals and marine life such as cobalt-blue starfish and pygmy seahorses.

The azure waters of Moalboal in Cebu ~ Keep your eyes peeled for other marine life ~ Snorkel among sparkling sardines

Those Tricky Sardines

The sardines often create spherical shapes known as bait balls in order to trick their predators. And, conveniently for spectators, they rise close to the ocean's surface to stay warm and to feed on plankton.

MA'IN HOT SPRINGS

Far more than just an oasis in the desert, these mineral hot springs are a relaxing and restorative retreat known since biblical times.

In the hills of central western Jordan, at an elevation of 264m (866ft) below sea level – about 200m (656ft) above the nearby Dead Sea – Hammamat Ma'in, as it is known to locals, is more than a dozen hot springs that cascade down a rocky ledge and into terraced pools frequented by locals and tourists alike. It's a famous oasis of waterfalls and cliffside baths set in a gorgeous canyon filled with palm trees and striking travertine formations.

These days, the majority of the hot springs and waterfall pools have been walled off for use by the guests of the upscale Ma'in Hot Springs Resort & Spa, which offers a wide range of treatments such as mud facials and wraps, underwater massages and more. However, there is also a public section where, for a fee, families relax in the pools and soak beneath the falling water. There are also shower facilities.

Country Jordan · **City** Madaba · **Type** hot springs · **Cost** JD15 · **Family friendly** yes

Soak in restorative springs known for their healing properties ~ A steaming waterfall at Ma'in Hot Springs

How long have these hot springs been around?

Ma'in has been known since biblical times, when it was called Belemounta, and its restorative hot springs and waterfalls are believed to have been frequented at least since the earliest days of Rome. Even the likes of Herod the Great are said to have appreciated a hot soak.

Are the waters therapeutic?

The mineral-rich water at Ma'in contains elements like calcium, chloride, magnesium, potassium, radon, sodium, hydrogen sulfide and carbon dioxide, all of which are known for their healing properties.

How hot is the water?

It has some of the hottest hot springs in Jordan, between 40°C (104°F) and 63°C (145°F).

What bathing costume should I wear?

The people of Jordan are mostly Muslim and dress fairly conservatively. Modest swimwear is advised, as is light footwear for use on sun-roasted rock surfaces.

Healing Hot Springs

Natural hot springs are an important part of medical tourism, or travel to find medical treatment not found or affordable at home. This is usually for people needing treatment against chronic ailments like bone, joint and muscle pain, and skin and circulatory diseases. Ma'in's waters are known for their curative characteristics.

BIG LAGOON

Kayak on the turquoise waters of the Philippines' most iconic natural lagoon.

Big in size and impact, this cerulean 'marine lake' surrounded by towering limestone cliffs is one of the most defining aerial images of Palawan Province. It's most commonly visited on the 'Tour A' island-hopping day trip run by various operators in El Nido. The lagoon rules dictate that tour boats moor in deeper waters outside the long, shallow channel that connects the lagoon to the ocean. From here, visitors have the option of kayaking or swimming into the lagoon. While you can stand up when you move further into the channel, opting for a kayak makes it much easier to explore and admire the interior 'lake'. You can also pull your kayak onto a handful of tiny beaches in the channel if you fancy taking a dip. With visitor numbers now restricted by the number of kayaks available (50), you may have to queue for a while, but it's absolutely worth it.

Country Philippines · **Region** Palawan · **Type** lagoon · **Cost** kayak rental P250 · **Activities** kayaking · **Family friendly:** children must be able to sit in a kayak

Letting it all go at the Big Lagoon

THE JOY OF WATER

Should I bring my snorkel?
The channel is sandy and the main lagoon is quite deep in most sections, so there's not a lot to see underwater.

Can I use my drone here?
As long as you're comfortable launching and landing your drone from your kayak, or from one of the tiny beaches in the channel, go to town. Be mindful that the high cliffs can interfere with the GPS signal.

Isn't there another lagoon around here?
In the next bay around you'll find Small Lagoon, a smaller but also spectacular version of its more famous twin.

Do I have to wear a life jacket?
Yes, they're mandatory.

Can I stay here?
Yes! The luxe Miniloc Island is the only resort on the lagoon's island.

Say No to Plastic

In September 2018, El Nido banned plastic bottles, bags and other single-use plastics on boat tours, so don't forget to bring your reusable water bottle. Purified water is provided on tour boats.

BEITOU

The volcanic valley of Beitou, a 30-minute ride on the metro from central Taipei, is brimming with hot-spring resorts promising a soothing soak.

This sleepy Taipei suburb's famous hot springs are fuelled by geothermal activity from the dormant Datun volcano group to its northeast. As you pull into Xinbeitou metro station, the telltale tang of sulphur hangs in the air. Disembark and start exploring; a brook winding through the main park exhales streams of steam, lending this place an otherworldly atmosphere. Fringed with forested hills and dotted with Japanese-era (1895-1945) villas, Beitou's spa status is spiced with romance and history.

You can choose between private tubs, outdoor Jacuzzis, tea- and flower-infused pools and traditional baths hewn from stone. The water, which can be baby-friendly warm or skin-blushingly hot, is restorative and healing. Come late afternoon and opt for one of the resorts on the hillside to enjoy the valley painted purple-maroon by the sunset from within your hot tub or lounging on a tatami mat sipping tea.

Country Taiwan · **City** Taipei · **Type** hot springs · **Cost** depends on resort, some are free · **Family friendly** yes

Stroll through the steaming town of Beitou ~ Admire the traditional architecture ~ Enjoy some time out ~ Join the locals for a dip

Is it expensive?

Beitou is brilliant because it caters to all wallets. You can splash out at luxury spas like Villa 32 or the historical Marshall Zen Garden; take the family to the mid-range Spring City Resort; or slither into a public bath for little more than a couple of dollars – Long Nice Hot Springs (in business since 1907) and the outdoor Millennium Hot Springs are two that come to mind.

Does the water really have healing properties?

So they say! The green, white or reddish waters (according to mineral make-up) are said to ease aching joints, cure skin problems and alleviate gout. At the very least, the heat works itself into tired muscles and rustles in a good night's sleep.

Do I have to get naked in public?

For the Japanese style, yes. But then everyone's naked and it's sex segregated so no need to be shy. Once you're in the water, your body is a blur anyway. Most people don't bat an eyelid, but you may get a few curious looks.

Hot-Spring Etiquette

Most public springs require you to wear a bathing cap or tie up your hair. Scrub your body in the public showers before entering the water. Embarrassingly, locals will remind you if you forget. If there's a bucket next to the pool, use this to splash your feet extra clean.

WADI SHAB

Escape the desert heat at this idyllic oasis hidden in one of Oman's most spectacular wadis.

One of the most scenic natural springs in all of Oman, Wadi Shab is also one of the most fun to find. The adventure begins with a 1¾-hour drive south of Muscat to the seaside town of Tiwi (hint: set off early) where you can safely park your hire car under the Wadi Shab bridge. You must then take a two-minute boat taxi across the water flowing through the wadi (valley) from where it's a 40-minute hike through a stunning wadi studded with lush date palms and turquoise pools to reach the designated swimming area – an idyllic cluster of freshwater pools. The first pool is quite shallow, perfect for less confident swimmers. From here you can wade upstream to the next, deeper pool, and then swim to a third. Strong swimmers can also access a small waterfall in a small cave beyond.

Country Oman · **Town** Tiwi · **Type** natural pool · **Family friendly** best suited to travellers with school-aged kids

Getting to this natural oasis is half the fun

THE JOY OF WATER

Is the water safe to drink?
Gushing from a natural spring, the water looks clean enough, but it's not drinkable.

What should I bring?
There's no tourism infrastructure in the wadi, so bring plenty of drinking water, snacks, sunscreen, comfortable walking shoes for the hike, and a waterproof case or dry bag for your valuables if you're keen to explore upstream, as it's not wise to leave valuables unattended.

Do I need reef shoes?
While not essential, reef shoes will come in handy here as the stones on the bottom of the stream are a bit sharp.

Is there anything else to see at the pools?
Keep your eyes peeled for desert wildlife such as the endemic Jayakar's lizard, which can grow up to 60cm (24in).

Is there a good time to go?
Wadi Shab can be visited year-round, but gets busy on weekends, so aim for weekdays if you like your space.

Essential Info

Be sure to ask the boatman
what time the last boat leaves
(usually 5pm) and leave plenty of
time for the hike back, or you may
get stranded overnight. Note that the
poorly maintained public toilet near
the boat dock is the only toilet
facility in the wadi.

EUROPE

© REDA&CO/Contributor | Getty Images

PAMUKKALE

Bathe like Cleopatra in frost-white travertines, filled with azure-blue thermal waters that spill spectacularly down a hillside in southwestern Turkey.

Pamukkale looks like the figment of a child's vivid imagination: snow-white calcite travertines drip down a steep sided valley like frosting on a fancy cake. The tiered pools are filled with warm, mineral-rich thermal water that shimmers like sky-blue topaz. Translating as 'cotton castle', Pamukkale borders on the celestial and the surreal. This is fantasy bathing at its best. But it's no secret: these terraced basins and petrified waterfalls hold more than two million visitors in their thrall each year. When you see it for real, you'll understand why.

The secret is dodging the crowds. Stay overnight in the village of Pamukkale to catch the early morning calm in the travertines, where you can bathe beneath a flawless sky and look out across the green valley rolling to mountains beyond. Though cooler, winter here is glorious as visitor numbers reduce to a trickle, especially on weekdays, making the pools at their quietest and most captivating.

Country Turkey • **Region** Aegean Coast • **Type** hot springs • **Cost** travertines 35 TL, Cleopatra's Pool 50 TL • **Family friendly** yes

Relax in the radon-rich Cleopatra's Pool ~ Take to the terraces ~ The snow-white travertines at this 'cotton castle' ~ Escape the crowds with an early morning visit

What's the best way to experience Pamukkale?

Hire a car to explore at your own pace and preferably stay overnight in the village to avoid the midday and afternoon rush. The walk down the travertines takes around 30 minutes, but factor in plenty of time for bathing.

What should I bring?

Shorts or a bathing suit, plus a towel, sunscreen (light reflects off the white surfaces making it easy to burn), water and snacks. In the travertines you'll need to go barefoot and carry your shoes. The ridges aren't as rough as they look because of the water flow, but take care not to slip.

How deep are the terrace pools?

They are deep enough to get fully submerged. The water is warm but not too hot, so still pleasant even on blisteringly hot summer days.

What's Cleopatra's Pool?

Legend has it that Cleopatra herself swam in the hot-spring-fed pool situated just above the travertines (hence the name).

Hierapolis

Pamukkale shares Unesco World Heritage status with the neighbouring Greek-Roman city of Hierapolis, founded by the bath-loving kings of Pergamon in the 2nd century BC. For a double hit of natural wonder and ancient history, follow a morning spent at Pamukkale with a visit to these remarkably well-preserved bath, temple and theatre ruins.

GOLDEN BEACH (ALTIN KUM)

Far from the beach umbrellas and banana boats, Cyprus's Golden Beach is the Med as it was before package tourism: just sand, surf, sun and silence.

Even before Cyprus was split in two, the Karpas Peninsula felt like the end of the world: a long, jutting isthmus, sprinkled with wild beaches, pointing like a finger across the Mediterranean. Despite the arrival of a handful of rustic beach cabins and the odd bit of flotsam and jetsam, not much has changed.

As you wander barefoot between the dunes at Golden Beach, with wild thyme perfuming the breeze, you may well have all 4km (2.5 miles) of sand to yourself, with perhaps a visiting sea turtle for company. Cypriot families come for weekend picnics, but on a weekday, an early morning swim feels like swimming off the map: nobody knows you are here, and the only sound is the gentle swish of waves and the rustle of sand grains skittering across the dunes. As you plunge into the Mediterranean, the sudden rush of noise and sensation is like waking from a dream.

Country Cyprus · **Region** Dipkarpaz (Rizokarpaso), Karpas Peninsula · **Type** beach · **Family friendly** yes

Wander the long stretch of sand at glorious Golden Beach

© Dmitry Pichugin | Shutterstock

Turtle Nesting Season

From June to August, loggerhead and green turtles haul themselves out onto the sand to lay their eggs, as they have since prehistoric times. Visit in August and September and you may see tiny hatchlings wriggling out of the sand and skittering over the dunes towards the surf.

Why is Golden Beach so undeveloped?
Geography, as much as anything else. Water is limited and access is via a dirt track, limiting the opportunities for resort development. In season, you can stay in basic wooden cabins and enjoy grilled fish and a cold beer as the sun dips behind the dunes, but that's the extent of it.

Is wild swimming safe here?
There are no lifeguards here, so you are on your own, but the currents are mild and the beach slopes gently.

When is the best time to visit?
Weekends see family picnics, and groups make stops in peak season, but come in late spring or early autumn and you may be the only person on the sand. Visit on a weekday for the maximum chance of serene silence.

What else is there in the area?
Beyond the beach, the coast becomes rocky and a rough road skirts past the ancient Apostolos Andreas monastery to the very end of the isthmus; from here, the next landfall is the coast of Syria.

PUNTING ON THE CAM

Take to the waters of one of the most winsome and storied stretches of river in Britain aboard the quirky crafts known as punts.

It is among the very oddest and oldest pleasure-boating traditions. Punting – propelling a keel-less flat-bottomed wooden boat via a long pole pushed against the riverbed – became a thing on the Thames in the 1860s. But it was on the shallow Cam, blessed with a fetching city-centre section of river and another just beyond city limits leading to the pretty, pub-rich parish of Grantchester, that punting for fun took off.

Plump for either a lower city length of river called the College Backs for the famous college grounds it abuts or the upper length out through countryside to Grantchester. You and the crew can navigate the Cam yourselves or take a tour. The former, despite occasional punt collisions, is more challenging but more fun, the latter saves embarrassment. Both have you meandering past historic colleges and manicured parklands around one of the planet's greatest centres of learning. Oar-inspiring.

Country England · **City** Cambridge · **Type** river · **Cost** 45-minute private tour £19 per adult (7-person minimum); one-hour hire £33 · **Family friendly** yes

Explore the rich history of the city ~ Admire Cambridge's architecture ~ Hope you can stay dry! ~ Punts waiting for passengers

So punting is a historic activity?

The punt was originally designed for carrying cargo. But 19th-century technological advances soon meant it was good for nothing more than having water-based capers in. The Cambridge University–based Damper Club oversaw punting on the Cam from late-Victorian times until the 1980s; the membership requirement was that you had unwillingly fallen into the river fully clothed. Scudamore's, the country's original punting company, still operates on the Cam today. Suffice it to say that punting is a rite of passage for everyone, resident and visitor alike, who spends time in Cambridge.

How do I punt?

First, stand at the back of the boat, not the front as on Oxford punts! Get a balanced stance. The rear foot should be slightly closer to your preferred punting side. Lift the pole, then slide it down the boat's outside level with your rear foot until it touches the riverbed. Hand-over-hand, push on the pole. Lift-off!

"Jack Scudamore pioneered Cambridge pleasure-punting in the Edwardian period. The activity proved extremely popular for both residents and university pupils, with many regularly taking to the water for relaxation, inspiration or frolics. Eight colleges grace the private banks of this 1.6km (1 mile) stretch of river, widely regarded to be one of the most beautiful."

Ivan Krushkov, Scudamore's Punting Company

BAD GASTEIN

Feel the restorative powers of radon in the richly mineral thermal waters of Bad Gastein, high in Austria's glacier-capped Hohe Tauern Alps.

Arriving in Bad Gastein is like drifting gently back in time to the belle époque and the dawning era of European spas, when only royalty, aristocracy and the seriously loaded could afford to plunge into its healing waters. The town is ringed by snow-capped peaks, sitting 1000m (3280ft) above sea level and riven by the thunderous Gasteiner Ache falls – there are few backdrops more striking for a *Wasserkur* (water cure). And the force of water is felt keenly everywhere.

Local medical centres, hotel spas and public baths tap directly into the curative, radon-laced hot springs. Slip into a private radon bath and after just minutes you'll notice a deep, penetrative inner heat begin to tease out tension. More magical still, perhaps, are the open-air thermal baths, where you can float in rejuvenating waters while gazing up at Alpine peaks, which glow pearlescent by night as if lit from within.

Country Austria • **Region** Salzburgerland • **Type** hot springs • **Cost** fees for the spas and medical centres vary • **Family Friendly** yes

What's so special about the water?
Glacial water trickles down from the Hohe Tauern Alps, where it heats to temperatures of between 44°C (111°F) and 47°C (116°F) around 2000m (6562ft) below the earth's surface. Some five million litres a day gush forth at 18 different springs.

Where can I bathe?
Many hotels pump in the water and offer private baths. There are two public spas, complete with outdoor pools and hydromassage: the central Felsentherme and the Alpentherme in nearby Bad Hofgastein.

What's all the fuss about radon?
This natural gas is at optimal levels for healing here. The water is said to alleviate rheumatism and respiratory ailments, stop inflammation, stimulate circulation and stabilise the immune system.

Can I drink the stuff?
In moderation. There's a free drinking fountain in town (ask locals to point you towards the *Trinkbrunnen*). Bring your own bottle.

The outdoor pool at Felsentherme ~ Water gushes everywhere here ~ Explore the stunning scenery

Water to Inspire

In the late 19th century, composer Johann Strauss and Empress Elisabeth (Sisi) both put the benefits of Bad Gastein's waters to the test; the empress was so impressed that she penned a poem in 1886 beginning: 'Only sick bones I thought of bringing, where mystically your hot water springs...' Schubert and Klimt were apparently also fans.

HAMPSTEAD HEATH BATHING PONDS

These cold-water reservoirs in the rolling woodlands of London's Hampstead Heath are the antidote to city living.

In a city as chaotic and noisy as London, it's remarkable to find yourself taking an icy cold dip in the tranquillity of one of Hampstead Heath's swimming ponds with only the clouds above and local ducks for company. Everything about swimming at Hampstead Heath feels utterly magical, like you've been transported back in time to a London of old: people are friendly, mobile phones are banned and conditions are rustic.

Hampstead has three different swimming ponds – the Kenwood Ladies' Pond; nearby, the Men's Pond; and on the west side of the heath, the Mixed Swimming Pond – each quite different from the others. Arguably, the Ladies' Pond offers the best experience (sorry lads) with the pond set in a treed garden providing privacy for ladies who like to spend the afternoon reading, sunbathing or picnicking with friends, as well as wild swimming in the city.

Country England · **City** London · **Type** manmade reservoirs · **Cost** £2 · **Family friendly** no

Take care diving as water levels fluctuate ~ Strolling through the park to the ponds ~ Join the locals for a refreshing dip ~ Brace yourself for the chilly water

How deep are the ponds?
That varies by pond, but you can't touch the bottom!

Is there somewhere to put my things?
Don't take valuables as your towel and bag are left at your own risk, though theft is not common here.

Will it be crowded?
In the height of summer, yes it is. You can expect to queue for up to an hour during peak times (the afternoon on a hot London day), but any other day (the rest of the year, and especially in winter) it's very peaceful and tucked away from the tourist hordes.

I'm not a confident swimmer, how safe is it?
Alas the ponds are not for you. There are lifeguards, but the water is very deep and often very cold.

When are the ponds open?
It's mainly a summertime affair, but popular year-round including Christmas and New Year's Day (ice or snow are no match for committed pond swimmers).

Founded in 1928, the Highgate Diving Club was based at the Men's Pond where Olympic-level high-platform diving was practised, entertaining onlookers with comical as well as acrobatic stunts. The high platform was removed years ago and now swimmers are discouraged from even diving in from the pontoons. With fluctuating water levels, safety is a real concern.

GROTTA AZZURRA

Be lulled by a singing captain as you drift into Capri's ethereally lovely sea cavern, where Roman emperors once worshipped waters of bluest blue.

The oars of the rowboat slide gently into a luminescent sea of startling lapis lazuli. The baritone voice of a 'singing captain' echoes off the rock walls as silvery light flickers on the water's surface. For a brief moment the world outside ceases to exist. This is the Grotta Azzurra, or the Blue Grotto, rightfully the biggest crowd-puller on the chic island of Capri, marooned off the tip of Italy's fabled Amalfi Coast.

The water-loving Romans sure knew how to pick their secret spots. This brilliantly lit cavern was once the sacred sanctuary of Emperor Tiberius, who built a quay around it in AD 30, complete with a *nymphaeum* (shrine to the water nymph). The carved Roman landing stage is still visible to the rear of the cave and statues found here are now shown at the Casa Rossa in Anacapri. Some 2000 years (and countless superstitious sailors and fishermen) later, the grotto still hasn't lost its power to enchant.

Country Italy • **Region** Capri • **Type** natural sea grotto • **Cost** fee for the return boat trip • **Activities** boat ride, swimming • **Family friendly** yes

A secret spot favoured by the Romans ~ Witness the beauty of Capri's coastline ~ Gently glide by boat through this magical sea cave

How can I get here?
The easiest way to visit is to take a tour from Marina Grande. There's an additional fee for the four-person rowboat ride into the grotto. Allow a good hour. Singing captains are included in the price so don't feel obliged to tip them extra.

When should I go?
There are non-stop departures from 9am to 5pm. The light is at its dazzling blue best between noon and 2pm. Avoid visiting on an overcast day when the sunlight effect is less dramatic. From November to March, the cavern is often off-bounds due to choppy water and poor weather conditions.

How busy does it get?
Very, especially in the afternoon, so you'll need to be prepared to queue with the other rowboats waiting their turn to enter. July and August are prime time – shoulder seasons are slightly quieter.

Can I swim here?
Not in the cave itself, but you can swim just outside the entrance. Take care though as it can get choppy.

Why is the Water so Blue?

The cavern is said to have sunk in prehistoric times, blocking every opening except the 1.3m- (4.2ft-) high entrance, which is key to the magical blue light. Sunlight enters through a small underwater aperture and is refracted through the water; this combined with the reflection off the white sandy sea floor produces the vivid blue effect.

LANTIC BAY

Forego the crowds and crashing waves of North Cornwall and idle away an afternoon in the calm waters of South Cornwall's favourite hidden cove.

Summertime revellers in need of some R&R can rejoice: Lantic Bay acts as the perfect pit stop on your coastal adventures. Family friendly and yet relatively undiscovered, the protected cove can be located via a detour on an 11km (6.9 mile) coastal clifftop walk between model fishing villages Polruan and Polperro. Where North Cornwall's coast is known for its windswept surfing breaks, the southern shoreline promises unspoilt and sheltered sandy pockets dotted between charming neighbourhoods.

Viewed from the cliff walk, Lantic Bay is a vision of England's southern coast: a patch of sand and shingle, green-turquoise waters, rolling green hills and craggy rocks falling into the sea. After working up a sweat on your hike, clamber down to a satisfying – and refreshing – dip. After an afternoon drying off the saltwater in the sun, head off on your merry way beside unbeaten views of the Cornish coastline.

Country England · **Region** Cornwall · **Type** beach · **Family friendly** yes

Hike down craggy cliffs for a cooling splash at this hidden cove

THE JOY OF WATER

Right, how cold can I expect the water to be?
The beach is sheltered, but the water isn't warm even in summer. Think of it as assuredly invigorating, and consider bringing a wetsuit if visiting out of season.

Who's the beach best suited for?
The gentle lapping waves are perfect for paddling toddlers, fun-loving bathers or for those who'd prefer just to dip their toes in.

When's the best time to visit?
Aim for late summer into early autumn for the most comfortable water temperature, avoiding peak crowds of holiday-goers in July or August.

How long does the coastal walk take?
There's no rush in this part of the world. If you're up for the hike, the coastal footpath is well-marked and should take less than 2½ hours to walk the entire stretch. It gets a little steep in the gorse-strewn pathway down to the beach, so if need be, you can also reach the beach by car.

"Cornwall is special in so many ways but Lantic Bay is one of its many hidden gems. A break in stunning Southeast Cornwall is the best way to recharge the body and bring peace and wellbeing to all who visit."

Malcolm Bell, CEO Visit Cornwall.

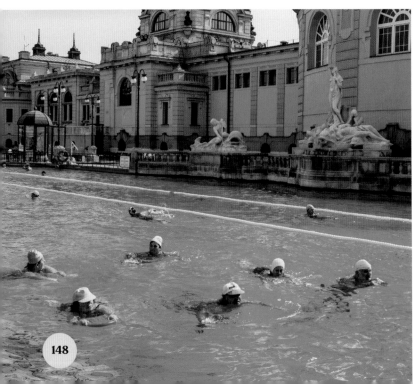

SZÉCHENYI BATHS

The crowning glory of Budapest's baths, Széchenyi is a paragon of turn-of-the-century spa architecture, encompassing 18 pools in sumptuous surrounds.

Europe's only major city to sit on thermal springs, Budapest has been a spa-going hotspot since Roman times. Around 120 founts of thermal water burst from a geological fault line beneath Hungary's handsome Danube-straddling capital, and a dozen bathhouses, built over the past four centuries, channel this into sophisticated bathing establishments popular with locals and visitors alike.

The one everyone wants to sample is Széchenyi. This is among the continent's biggest thermal pool complexes, ensconced in a mustard-yellow colonnaded edifice dating from 1913. Most hot water is inside, but come sun or snow, the appeal of the three magnificent outside pools endures. With waters permanently 27°C to 38°C (81°F to 100°F), poolside basking in summer or dipping away from below-zero air temperatures in winter are equally enjoyable.

Country Hungary • **City** Budapest • **Type** thermal baths • **Website** www.szechenyibath.hu • **Cost** 6300Ft • **Activities** bathing, sauna, massage, pedicure • **Family friendly** no

Soak in style ~ Grand interior details of the spa ~ Experience life as a Budapest local

Are the thermal baths a local experience or more for tourists?
Spa-going is an essential part of Budapest city culture, with people flocking to them to de-stress, luxuriate or play chess, and as natural for residents as the thermal waters themselves. To truly tap into the way life works here, you should visit a bathhouse.

Are the baths sex segregated?
Not all city baths are always mixed-sex, although Széchenyi has mixed-sex admittance daily.

What are the ticketing options?
There are sometimes baffling arrays of ticket options: the ticket covers cabin use and access to all pools for as long as desired on any one day.

What do I need to bring?
Bring your own towel and swimming costume, but do not bring non-essential items or valuables.

Are children welcome?
Széchenyi is aimed at adult bathers. Children over 14 are admitted.

What's in the Water?

The baths have magnesium, chloride, hydrocarbonate, calcium, bicarbonate and fluoride in their waters. These properties are thought to have numerous medicinal benefits. The hot springs heating the pools have temperatures of 74-77°C (165-171°F), which are cooled to make the actual water temperature 18-30°C (64-86°F) in the 15 inside pools and 27-38°C (81-100°F) in the three outside pools.

FELL CENTRE KIILOPÄÄ

Saunas are integral to Finland's heritage, but sweat is only half the story. In between sauna sessions Finns freshen up in icy natural waters.

Finns treat sauna time seriously. And while it is the image of a steam-filled, wood-panelled roomful of naked people that comes to mind when one imagines a Finnish sauna (that, indeed, is how it is), the real sauna ritual for Finns also entails an outdoors immersion in invariably icy pool or lake water for cooling off after each sweat-out.

Of course, the further north you venture in this Arctic country, the greater the urge to gravitate to the steam room. Lapland has many of Finland's most characterful saunas, but Fell Centre Kiilopää's ultra-traditional wood-smoke sauna is picture-perfect. Sweat to the scent of smoking birch twigs, then steel yourself for a soak in a Lappish pool so freezing it is bounded by deep snow most of the year and ice needs to be routinely broken from the surface. Forest and fells frame the background – this is Finland at its most quintessentially Finnish.

Country Finland · **Region** Lapland · **Type** ice pool · **Cost** €10/13 hotel guest/non-guest for sauna and pool · **Activities** wild swimming · **Family friendly** yes

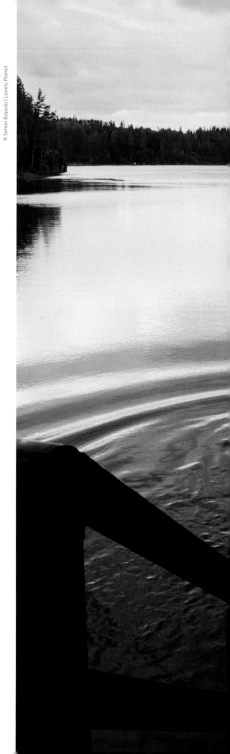

© Simon Bajada | Lonely Planet

Do as the Finns do and finish your sauna with a freezing dip

Saunas: an Answer for Everything

A sauna is more than mere relaxation for most Finns. Traditionally, saunas were the first rooms to be finished in a house. Political negotiations have been carried out in them. The word *löyly*, referencing the steam released in saunas, also means 'spirit' – there has long been a link between sauna-going and spirituality in Finland, too.

Must I be naked in a Finnish sauna?
For Finns, relaxing in a sauna naked is about the most natural pastime there is, so natural that saunas were traditionally the place of choice to give birth. From a Finnish perspective, all are equal in the nude in a roomful of steam. You will stick out more if you enter a sauna with a costume on than if you go with the flow and go unclothed.

Are they sex segregated?
A sauna will invariably be divided into men's and women's sections, but save your swimwear for putting on when you enter the common area outside, which is usually mixed sex. Keep your costume too for the shuddering plunge into the water.

Is it good for you?
Just don't linger too long in the 80°C (176°F) sauna or in the chilly water: it is a 75°C (167°F) temperature switch for your body. Finns swear by the health benefits of this fire-to-freeze contrast, but do not try being the brave newcomer by outdoing Finns at their own thing.

153

ST NECTAN'S GLEN

Take a bracing cold-water dip in a fabled fairy glen, with a series of plunge pools and waterfalls to explore.

Just along the coast from the clifftop castle of Tintagel, believed by some to be the legendary birthplace of King Arthur, this wooded glen is a place that feels steeped in myth and mysticism.

Hidden away in one of Cornwall's oldest areas of ancient oak woodland, there are three waterfalls to experience here, carved out from the slate by the River Trevillet. Most people head straight for the main one, St Nectan's Kieve, where the river has sliced through the rock to create an impressive 18m (59ft) waterfall and a deep kieve (an old Cornish word for basin). Draped with mosses, ferns and foliage, it's a dreamy spot that some believe to have mystical powers: you'll see ribbons, charms and crystals dotted around (it's also a favourite spot for pagan wedding ceremonies). A second waterfall clatters down above the main cascade, and a newly opened third can be accessed via a purpose-built boardwalk.

Country England · **Region** Cornwall · **Type** waterfall · **Website** www.st-nectansglen.co.uk · **Cost** £5.95 · **Activities** bathing, wild swimming · **Family friendly** yes

Coins left in a wishing tree ~ Ritual prayer ribbons ~ Waterfalls abound in St Nectans Glen ~ Couples taking part in a commitment ceremony

How cold is it?
Chilly – straight-from-the-cold-tap temperatures, unless there's been an unusually long period of warm weather.

How do I get here?
On the coast road from Tintagel to Boscastle (B3263), park in the free car park in Trethevy, and follow the signed trail. It's about a mile walk from the car park.

When is the best time to visit?
Avoid July and August, when the pools can be busy – aim for June or September, or if you're really brave, the depths of winter.

Can I bring my dog?
Yes, if it's well-behaved.

Who was St Nectan?
A 6th-century Irish holy man, the eldest of the 24 children of King Brychan of Brycheiniog (Brecknock in Wales). He is most associated with Hartland in Devon, where a church is dedicated to him, but he is believed to have built a hermitage in Cornwall.

Spirits of the Glen

Many spooky sightings have been experienced by people walking along the wooded valley to St Nectan's Glen, including ghostly monks, grey ladies and even the knights of King Arthur. It's also said to be frequented by a population of fairies and piskies (the Cornish word for pixies).

THERMAE BATH SPA

Bathe in Britain's only natural thermal waters while gazing over a bounty of hay-hued Georgian buildings in Unesco-listed Bath's city centre.

Bath was always the UK's biggest spa destination: at least since the Romans built a bathhouse here to take advantage of the piping hot waters arising from the Pennyquick geological fault at almost 50°C (122°F) and at rates of one million-odd litres daily, and dubbed the settlement *Aquae Sulis*. Today Thermae Bath Spa has the only naturally thermal and nutrient-rich waters for bathing in Britain.

The spa, which cleverly combines Georgian stonework with modern glass and metal across two sites, the 18th-century Cross Bath and newer New Royal Bath, blends in seamlessly with its historic surroundings. New Royal Bath even lets you survey them from its rooftop pool. Floating in 33°C (91°F) water with such a view is special even by the standards of the world's most spa-spangled nations. Work up to this warm-water wonder with a wallow in the spa's other thermal pool, the Minerva, on ground level, complete with lazy river.

Country England · **City** Bath · **Type** thermal baths · **Cost** from £36 per person · **Activities** bathing, sauna, Watsu, massage, body scrubs, facials · **Family friendly** No

Soak your bones at this historic thermal spa

Britain's Other Spa Towns

Bath might have had the only naturally occurring thermal waters, but wellness-seekers of times gone by in Britain had several resorts purporting to sport curative waters for the sampling: Royal Tunbridge Wells, Cheltenham, Great Malvern and Harrogate in England; Builth Wells, Llanwrtyd, Llangammarch and Llandrindod Wells in Wales; and Crieff Hydro and Strathpeffer in Scotland.

So can I bring the kids here?
Children under 16 are not allowed into the New Royal Bath, but ages 12 to 16 are allowed in the Cross Bath, which is essentially a one-level Georgian building enclosing a small pool.

I have tried the thermal pools but still have time left. What else can I do?
Thermae Bath Spa is a fully-fledged spa. In between the Minerva and rooftop pools there is space for both a wellness suite, included in standard thermal bath entry prices, and various treatments, which are extra. Most interesting among the treatments is Watsu, one-to-one aquatic therapy including shiatsu massage and acupressure.

I get that *aquae* is Latin for waters, but who was Sulis?
The Romans might have named Bath *Aquae Sulis* but Sulis was actually a Celtic deity who had been revered in Britain, and mainly in Bath, long before the first toga showed up on the shores. Sulis, the Celts' goddess of thermal water, was worshipped right on the site of the Cross Bath.

BALOS BEACH

Balos beach's lily-white sands and lapping turquoise waters draw the crowds to this remote stretch of Crete's rugged Gramvousa Peninsula.

It's a wonderfully wild setting for one of Crete's best-known beaches – tucked away on the Gramvousa Peninsula and backed by scrubby desolate hills. This might conjure images of a deserted beach devoid of sun-seekers, but nothing could be further from the truth. Balos graces the cover of countless tourist brochures for Crete, and beachgoers from far and wide make the trip out here to witness the stunning, raw natural beauty of this lagoon-beach in the flesh.

While it does suffer from overcrowding in the height of summer – particularly when the day trippers clamber off the cruise boat for a few precious hours to soak it all up – there's no denying the sheer beauty of its aquamarine shallow lagoon waters that blend with the pinkish hue of the sandy beach. When you get to see Balos in all of its glory on a perfect summer's day, it seems to be lifted straight from the pages of those tourist brochures.

Country Greece · **Region** Crete · **Type** beach · **Activities** swimming · **Family friendly** not really

Take in the views on the walk down ~ Small church on Gramvousa Peninsula ~ Crowds descend on this beauty of a beach ~ The boat arrives for Balos action

How do I get here?
It's not particularly easy. The options include hopping on a day cruise (May to October) from the town of Kissamos (Kastelli) or you can drive. It's a scenic, yet bone-shaking, 12km (7.5-mile) drive from the nearest village of Kalyviani to the beach car park, then a 1km (0.6-mile) walk down a path to the beach. You really need a 4WD.

Is there somewhere to buy food and drink?
Nope. There are no facilities at Balos, it's literally just a beach with some basic toilets. So pack a picnic or you can grab a bite at one of the excellent restaurants in Kalyviani. If you take the cruise boat you can buy food and drink on board.

If I opt for the cruise, how long will I have to enjoy Balos?
The cruise usually stops at the nearby offshore island of Imeri Gravousa for around 90 minutes where you can explore the hilltop Venetian fortress or take a dip. Then it stops at Balos for a few hours before making the trip back.

Travel Tips

If you're taking a day cruise to visit Balos, get to the ferry early to bag a seat as it packs out in summer and you'll be standing the entire trip. There is no shade at the beach but you can hire an umbrella/lounge there or from the ferry company.

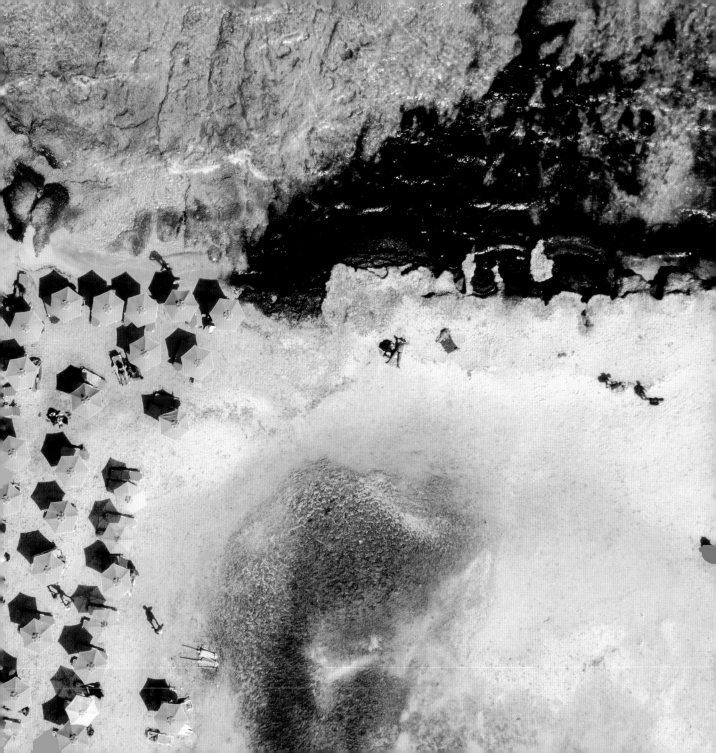

LLYN CAU

Nestled below Cader Idris, this ice-blue glacial lake is so spectacularly flanked by mountainside that for centuries it was believed to be a volcanic crater.

The place names in this scree-strewn tract of Snowdonia sparkle with evocativeness. Cader Idris (Cadair Idris), the 893m (2930 ft) high point of Southern Snowdonia translates as 'Chair of Idris' – with Idris either a 7th-century prince who vanquished the Irish on the mountain or a giant warrior-poet who created a rocky chair for himself here to stargaze. Both stories moodily conjure images of the broken, history-steeped summit that dominates this landscape and so enfolds Llyn Cau that the lake's own name means 'closed lake'.

The main lake approach is from the east, the only side not fortified with rock walls, but the best swimming is off the end in the shadow of Cader Idris via a gently shelving stony beach. Spread-eagled shoreline boulders also allow the energetic to throw themselves in. Icy this teal tarn is, but after the ascent to get here you may well be hot enough – and wowed enough – to plunge in.

Country Wales · **Region** Gwynedd · **Type** lake · **Activities** wild swimming · **Family friendly** yes

Brave an icy plunge into the water after working up a sweat to get here

The map says there is no road access. How do I get here?
The map is correct, but sometimes the most rewarding wild swims come after enduring a foot-slog first. Difficulty of access certainly keeps crowds down, too. The easiest way in is via the Minfford path, starting near the Minfford Inn at the junction of the A487/B4405. The other route is via the Pony Path, rising from the car park southwest of Llyn Gwernan on the Dolgellau side of the mountain, and goes via Cader Idris first. This way, you will see Llyn Cau directly and dramatically below you from the summit, and can pick up the Minfford path, which descends steeply to the lake.

How much time should I allow to spend at Llyn Cau?
Coming from the closest road access point on the Minfford Path, at least half a day. Walking to the lake and back takes a good couple of hours, and that is without exploring, taking a dip and munching a picnic (all three of which come highly recommended).

Where to Stay

Right up there with Wales' most special outdoor experiences, Llyn Cau and its surrounds are not to be seen in a rush. Prolong your visit by staying over a night or two. Dolgellau to the northeast, the Gwernan Lake Hotel to the north and the two lakeshore hotels in Tal-y-Llyn make good bases.

MÝVATN NATURE BATHS

Sink into the bath-warm waters of this geothermal-heated swimming pool while gazing over one of Iceland's most dramatic volcanic landscapes.

Iceland is a place of many eye-popping geological wonders, but its hot-water pools (known locally as 'hot pots') are a highlight for many visitors. Created by volcanic activity deep beneath Iceland's rocky crust, hot pots are scattered all over this otherworldly island. Some have been turned into swimming pools, the most famous of which is the Blue Lagoon, just outside Reykjavík.

Mývatn Nature Baths offers the same experience, but it's much less frequented. It's sited in one of Iceland's most geothermal-active areas, and the pool's waters originate 2500m (8202ft) underground, emerging at a temperature of around 130°C (266°F), before being piped into the baths at a more temperate 36°C to 40°C (97°F to 104°F). Lying back in the mica-blue water, surrounded by billowing clouds of steam as you look out over an extra-terrestrial landscape of geysers, fumaroles, volcanoes and lava fields, is a memorable experience.

Country Iceland · **Region** Mývatn · **Type** hot spring · **Cost** 4500kr/1800kr/free per adult/teenager/child · **Activities** bathing, steam baths · **Family friendly** yes

Doesn't get much more atmospheric ~ Steam rises up all over the countryside ~ Rock tunnel at Mývatn ~ Steaming mud pools abound ~ The landscape is otherwordly

Where does the water come from?
The lagoon's water comes from Iceland's National Power Company's borehole in Bjarnarflag.

How deep is the pool?
1.3m (4.2ft)

I've heard Icelanders like to bathe nude – do I have to bare all?
They do, but at Mývatn it's definitely bathing costumes on (there are kids in there, for heaven's sake).

Is the water good for the skin?
Supposedly. Mývatn's water is laced with a concoction of minerals, silicates and micro-organisms that are believed to have beneficial effects for many skin and respiratory conditions.

Should I worry about the chemicals?
No. The water at Mývatn is actually way healthier than a regular swimming pool: due to its chemical composition, bacteria and vegetation don't survive in it, making chloride and other disinfectants unnecessary.

Jóna Frímansdóttir lives near Mývatn and has been taking a regular dip in the baths for more than twenty years. "My favourite time to bathe is in the middle of winter, when it's freezing cold outside: it warms the soul as much as the body. Foreigners think we're mad, but people have been doing this in Iceland for the last thousand years."

Jóna Frímansdóttir,
local bather

FORTY FOOT

At this seaside-suburb plunge pool, redoubtable Dubliners brave daily dips in the Irish Sea and culture-seeking travellers soak up literary references.

When serendipity smiles and time, tide and sunlight conspire to transform the sea at Sandycove into a turquoise-tinted lagoon, then a dawn dip in the Forty Foot is the perfect start to a Dublin day. Such moments are all the more special for their rarity. Usually conditions are choppy and the water's complexion mirrors the mood of the irascible Irish sky. But whatever the weather, the Forty Foot is never dull.

Throughout summer, the pool hosts garrulous locals, laughing and leaping from rocks. Dubliners have been throwing themselves into the chilly embrace of the Irish Sea here for over 250 years.

This restless rockpool features in the work of some of Ireland's most celebrated writers, including James Joyce, who once resided in the Martello tower that overlooks the Forty Foot and chose this as the setting for the first scene in his magnum opus, *Ulysses*.

Country Ireland · **City** Dublin · **Type** sea bath · **Family friendly** yes

No skinny-dipping here! ~ Inspirational views ~ Bask in the literary history ~ Tough Dubliners swim year-round

Remind me, why would I jump into a sea described by Ireland's most revered wordsmith as 'snot green' and 'scrotumtightening'? Because it's a quintessential Dublin experience – a tradition stretching back two-and-a-half centuries. And some daily dippers claim the water has health-bestowing powers.

Does it get busy? On sunny summer days this suburban swimming spot is the Fair City's worst-kept secret. And, believe it or not, at Christmas there's often a queue.

Is it 40-feet deep? No. The backstory to the name has been forgotten, but popular theories suggest it stems from the 42nd Royal Highland Regiment of Foot (the 'Black Watch'), once based nearby, or the height of the Martello tower that overlooks it.

Anything else I should know? Look before you leap. It's tidal, and the depth varies. Don't dive.

Lurid Literary Mention

'The snot green sea. The scrotumtightening sea.' Buck Mulligan's lurid description of Dublin Bay on 16 June 1904 – as he contemplates the famous Forty Foot sea baths from a Martello tower in the opening pages of James Joyce's *Ulysses* – doesn't deter devotees of the modernist masterpiece from swimming at Sandycove.

CALA GOLORITZÈ

Find out what the fuss is about Sardinia's beaches at one of the fairest of all, Cala Goloritzè: a white-pebble cove sliding into surreally blue waters.

The sun blazes down on the otherworldly Golgo plateau, where wild goats, pigs and donkeys graze. It seems an unlikely spot to begin a trek to one of Italy's most sublime beaches. But as you pick your way along old mule trails that pass gnarled holm oak woods, fragrant Mediterranean scrub and sheepfolds, arresting views begin to open up of the glittering sea and sheer limestone cliffs honeycombed with caves. Then suddenly, there below, is Cala Goloritzè, a perfect half-moon of bone-white pebbles pummelled by a sea so ludicrously turquoise it looks Photoshopped.

But it's real all right. One joyous leap and you're feeling revived and elated in the shallow, deliciously cool, clear water, fed by underwater karst springs. You cast a glance up at the 500m- (1640ft-) high cliffs towering above you and the needle-thin rock spire of Monte Caroddi. Somehow the word *bella* (beautiful) doesn't quite cut it.

Country Italy • **Region** Sardinia • **Type** beach • **Activities** swimming, snorkelling, hiking, free climbing • **Family friendly** yes

THE JOY OF WATER

Say hi to the locals on your trek to the beach ~ Don't worry about working up a sweat – you'll soon be cooling off at one of Italy's best beaches. ~ Sublime Sardinia. It doesn't get much better than this! ~ Take in the spectacular turquoise waters of Cala Goloritzé

Where exactly is Cala Goloritzè?
The bay nestles in the southern crook of Sardinia's Golfo di Orosei, a sweeping crescent where the mountains collide with the sea.

How can I reach it?
Drive to the nearby town of Baunei, then follow the signs to the Altopiano del Golgo. It's a 15-minute drive north to Su Porteddu car park, the trailhead for the hike to the bay.

How's the walk?
It's a lovely 7km (4-mile) return hike through a wooded ravine (allow an hour down and an hour-and-a-half up). Bring a sunhat, sunscreen, sturdy shoes, plenty of water and snacks, and try to avoid the midday sun.

Is the water warm?
The water is a tad cooler than at some other Sardinian beaches, but this is a blessing in summer! That's because freshwater springs bubble up from the rocks at nearby Spiaggia delle Sorgenti. Bring a snorkel as the sea is incredibly clear.

Boating the Blue Crescent

If you do nothing else in Sardinia, boat it along the 20km (12-mile) southern stretch of the Golfo di Orosei. Here limestone cliffs plunge headlong into the sea, scalloped by sublime beaches, coves and grottoes. Coming from Cala Gonone, you'll tick off beauties like Cala Mariolu, Cala dei Gabbiani, and Cala Biriola. One reliable operator is Escursioni Cala Gonone.

SPIAGGIA DI PORTO GHIACCIOLO

A glorious little bay with luminous turquoise sea is overlooked by the sand-coloured abbey of Santo Stephano.

Porto Ghiacciolo is a tiny hoop of bay reached along a narrow, dusty, drivable track. Either side is fringed by greenery, and reaching the end, you discover the perfect small bay, a public beach, so you don't have to pay to sit here in summer (unusual as many Puglian beaches are colonised by beach clubs in July and August). Dive into the sparkling blue water, and you'll discover its secret: there's a freshwater spring feeding the sea at this point, so the water is always icy cold, hence its name 'icicle port'. In Puglia's summer months, as the sun belts down, it's an incredible feeling to experience this tingling chill, and if you walk out along the rocks you can leap into fabulously gin-clear water from the rocks. Plunge into the enveloping sea from one of the sea crags, and go snorkelling to spot dappled shoals of fish.

Country Italy · **Region** Puglia · **Type** beach · **Activities** swimming, snorkelling · **Family friendly** yes

The crystal-clear water here makes for excellent snorkelling

"We stay every summer in Polignano, and it was my local friend Paolo who showed me this small, almost unknown inlet called Porto Ghiacciolo. We had *ricci di mare* [sea urchin] with chilled white wine in an improvised restaurant on the shore, under the severe scrutiny of l'Abbazia [the convent on the promontory]."

Nicola Comiotto,
Head of Procurement, Nestlé

How do I get here?
It's a little under 5km (3 miles) by road southeast along the coast from Monopoli. There's no bus service here, so it's easiest to reach by car.

Are there any buildings nearby?
Yes, there's one large house set back from the beach, and there's a small bar-café on the beach for you to buy your glass of prosecco or *caffè in ghiaccio* (iced espresso coffee with almond milk) to feel like you're really living the *dolce vita* (sweet life).

What might I see when snorkelling?
Corals, crustaceans, octopuses and shoal upon shoal of glittering striped donzelle.

Is the water rough?
If it's a windy day, the waves will crash on the shore, a dramatic sight. On a calm day the sea is silkily calm.

How's the temperature?
This is the special feature of this beach, that the water always feels icy cool, even on the hottest day.

SATURNIA

Bathe just like the beauty-conscious Greeks and Romans did in the sulphuric waterfalls of Saturnia.

Driving along the backcountry lanes of the Maremma in southern Tuscany, where cypress-lined wheat fields give way to olive groves and wooded hillsides, the last thing you expect to stumble across is Saturnia. In a sudden burst, the surreal phosphorescent turquoise waters of these hot springs appear to light up the landscape, cascading into pools of pale travertine stone that drip like melted candlewax down to the river Albegna.

How tempting it is to jump in. So that's precisely what you do, ignoring the pong of rotten eggs bubbling up from these steamy, sulphur-rich waters, bath-warm at 37.5°C (99.5°F). You're by no means the first to marvel at these wild thermal baths in a crater at the foot of Mt Amiata: the Greeks were here first, then the Romans. Still today, everyone who makes it here raves about their beauty, and how their healing waters can ease aching joints and make the skin baby-soft.

Country Italy • **Region** Tuscany • **Type** hot springs • **Cost** free to bathe in springs, fees for treatments at the nearby spa • **Family friendly** Yes

Take a sulphuric soak for baby-soft skin

THE JOY OF WATER

Where can I swim?
Take the SP10 road to Cascata del Mulino, around 4km (2.5 miles) south of the walled hill town of Saturnia. Here the falls are free and deliciously wild.

What should I bring?
Bring bathers, a large towel and waterproof shoes as it can get rough underfoot, as well as sun lotion (there's precious little shade). Remember to remove jewellery: the sulphur in the water tarnishes gold and silver.

When's the best time to go?
Avoid peak season (July and August) when the baths are at their busiest. Early morning is less crowded, and sunset is just beautiful.

Is there somewhere to cool off?
Yes. If you're finding the hot springs too steamy on a scorching summer day, you can cool off in the river Albegna.

Isn't there also a spa?
The spa resort, Terme di Saturnia, just north of the falls, ups the luxury considerably, with pools, hydromassage, and treatments such as fango thermal mud packs.

Legendary Beginnings

Lore has it that Saturnia is named after the Roman god of agriculture, who grew weary with the constant wars on earth. In a bid to pacify mankind, he sent down a thunderbolt to create a deep rift where an enchanted spring of warm, sulphuric water would flow.

ST PETER'S POOL

This lozenge-shaped natural lido wraps around a sea of blue-green. Jumping here from various heights is a thing, depending on how brave you're feeling.

The craggily coasted island of Malta has many hidden bays and coves, but this secret-feeling sea pool is special. First, the sea. It's as blue as Paul Newman's eyes, or an indigo sari, drying on a beach. This is one of the surprisingly middle-of-nowhere places on the small island, approached along a rocky track, with a small trail of those in-the-know coming and going.

The scoop of coast has hollowed out into a natural, oval pool, surrounded by a high flat shelf of rock where you can lie out and bask like a lizard. To get there you have to abandon your car and walk. Locals bring barbecues and beers to accompany the drama of the sunset, and teens show off their jumping skills from the rocky plateaus around the edge.

Country Malta • **Town** Marsaxlokk • **Type** natural pool • **Activities** wild swimming • **Family friendly** yes

Show off your jumping skills at this fabulous natural pool

© simon leigh | Alamy Stock Photo, © sosn-a | Shutterstock (following page)

THE JOY OF WATER

What's the approach like?
You can drive the narrow road towards the pool, but will need to park up and walk the last section. The lane only takes one car at a time so you may have to reverse up if it's a busy time of year (the hot summer months). The closest bus stop is 2km (1.2 miles) away, but you can also reach here by water taxi from Marsaxlokk (you'll need to book a return time).

Is the water rough?
No, the pool is sheltered by the rocks, so it's usually calm.

How's the temperature?
The water is deep here and this is a Mediterranean island, so it's cool without being brain-freeze cold.

Is it good for jumping?
This is what being here is all about.

Is there shallow water?
The pool is deep, so isn't ideal for young children, though if you have inflatables it's manageable. It's better for confident swimmers.

"Jumping off the highest rock at St Peter's Pool was like a rite of passage during our long, lazy childhood summers in Malta, hitting the water with such force, emerging, victorious, to admire the rock towering above us."

Carrie Hindmarsh,
Founding Partner, Charabanc

BAY OF KOTOR

Swap the walled city of Kotor for neighbouring Dobrota where the mountains plunge into the sea, creating an unrivalled backdrop for a swim.

The small town of Dobrota is interspersed with opportunities to jump (or step) in to the refreshing Adriatic Sea. Neighbouring Kotor can get busy and hot – a single cruise ship can saturate this tiny city in an instant – but less-crowded Dobrota lies just 4km (2.5 miles) away along the Bay of Kotor. There's little development there – just a scattering of small cafes, rustic sand-coloured apartments and a quiet road – meaning there are few obstacles between you and the water.

The dramatic juxtaposition of the Dinaric Alps stretching as far as the eye can see sloping straight into the vast expanse of dark blue water makes it difficult to refuse a cool dip. Luckily Dobrota makes it easy, there are numerous steps leading into the water dotted along the shoreline – all 5km (3 miles) of it. If you'd rather get the shock of the cold water over with, you can jump or dive in places, too.

Country Montenegro · **Region** Dobrota · **Type** bay · **Activities** wild swimming · **Family friendly** yes

Alps views with your swim ~ Church tower overlooking the bay ~ Incredible views across Kotor Bay ~ Sunbathe to a scenic backdrop

How cold is it?
The water can get cold – around 14°C (57°F) from January to April – but rest assured fair-weather swimmers, it can reach up to 26°C (79°F) in August.

Is it busy?
In the summer months and holidays the shoreline can fill up with locals and tourists sunning themselves on any given surface, but there is so much water that you'd be hard pressed not to find a spot all for yourself.

Can I snorkel?
The Bay of Kotor isn't known for snorkelling and there aren't any organised tours, but that's not to say that you won't spot anything if you bring your own mask.

Can I get a well-earned drink after my swim?
There are a handful of small cafes and restaurants in Dobrota, most of which look out over the water. There are some great outdoor seating areas perfect for recuperating with a cheap beer.

What is the Bay of Kotor?

The Bay of Kotor is often described as a fjord but it is in fact a submerged river canyon. The narrowest part is a 4km- (2.5-mile-) wide channel in the south and the surrounding mountains reach up to an altitude of 1000m (3281ft).

FAIRY POOLS

Follow a well-trodden island trail along the course of the River Brittle to a series of swimming pools straight out of a Celtic fairy tale.

In the shadow of the mighty Cuillin Hills, the knife-edge mountains that cut across the heart of Skye, this chain of china-blue pools have been gouged out over the course of countless millennia by the clattering Brittle. Accessed via a trail that winds down through quintessential Skye scenery into a picturesque glen, here the river fractures into a string of mini-waterfalls, creating numerous plunge pools where brave bathers can slip into the bracing Scottish water for a heart-stopping but unforgettable dip. They look at their most picturesque on a clear day, when the water reflects the porcelain-blue sky, and you can see all the way down to the boulder-covered bottom. But don't be put off if it's raining: the pools will almost certainly be much quieter, the waterfalls may be more impressive (especially if it's rained for a few days), and you'll see whirls and eddies at work around the base of the cascades.

Country Scotland • **Region** Glenbrittle, Skye • **Type** natural pools • **Activities** bathing, wild swimming • **Family friendly** yes

Take your pick of natural pools ~ Head out on the water on a kayak tour ~ Scenery straight from a fairy tale

How long is the trail down to the pools?
About 2.4km (1.5 miles), via a mostly gravel path with some rocky sections.

How cold are the pools?
On a warm day: very chilly. On a cold day: positively hypothermic. You'll be thankful of a wetsuit at any time of year, but especially outside summer.

When's the best time to go?
Unfortunately, along with the rest of Skye, the Fairy Pools have suffered from social media overload. July and August are now a riot: consider May, June, September or October for more peace.

Is there car parking?
Yes, but you'll be very lucky to find a space in summer. Arrive early or late, come on a cloudy day and, most importantly of all, avoid July and August altogether.

Are there any loos or changing facilities?
There's a toilet at the Glenbrittle Campsite Cafe, where you can also warm yourself up with coffee and hot chocolate at the Cuillin Coffee Co.

"Our campsite is located at the foot of the Black Cuillin on Glenbrittle Beach. Everyone knows about the Fairy Pools nowadays, but we have many other wild swimming spots on our doorstep, from Corie Loch Lagan to Loch Brittle, including numerous waterfalls and four small lochs, three over 300m (984ft)."

Michelle Scott, Glenbrittle Campsite Manager

SANDWOOD BAY

Britain's remotest sandy beach separates Sandwood Loch and the tempestuous thrust of the Atlantic with its bedazzling ochreish sands and colossal dunes.

It is a humbling arrival for the traveller at Sandwood Bay after the two-hour traipse from the closest road: skittering path has replaced track, heathery moor has replaced cultivated land. Tumbledown ruins of farmsteads that failed to eke out an existence here are the only signs of humankind's meddling with this raw nature. You hear the crash of surf before you spy the bay. Next, a dramatic crest of dunes appears, dividing a shallow, snaking freshwater loch, prized for its trout, and the seething salty surf, which fans out along a 1.6km (1-mile) arc of beach.

Both loch and sea have gently shelving approaches, but tides can be vicious, meaning venturing out beyond toe-brushing distance of the seabed is for the experienced only. Off the southern end of the bay the sandstone sea stack of Am Buachaille sheers up in one of Scotland's most coveted deep-water solos, while the dunes are popular with wild campers.

Country Scotland · **Region** Sutherland · **Type** beach · **Activities** wild swimming, surfing, wild camping · **Family friendly** yes

Easy to see where it gets its name

How hard is the hike to get here?
The closest vehicular access is at the hamlet of Blairmore, from where a decent, easy-to-follow route runs on tracks and then paths 6.5km (4 miles) to Sandwood Bay. The going is fairly flat, and anyone used to walking, older children included, should find the path straightforward. Bear in mind that the outward route must be used to return, making for a 13km (8-mile) walk altogether.

Is it safe for kids to swim?
Watch your children vigilantly when they go in the water, which thanks to the Gulf Stream is not (quite) as chilly as you might think this far north, albeit nevertheless pretty cold. The sand gradient, on the beach and for the first few metres underwater, is gradual, so children can splash out a fair distance safely. But do not let them get out of their depth, and be immediately on hand to help if need be. The waves break a way offshore, but they are very wild and the undertow can be strong.

Cape Wrath

Sandwood Bay's splendid isolation is largely due to Cape Wrath, more than 259 sq km (100 sq miles) of wild, roadless headland surrounding the bay. Access to this wilderness is by foot from Sandwood Bay or by boat-bus combo from the Kyle of Durness, with the goal of most visitors being the lighthouse marking mainland Britain's most northwesterly point.

LAKE BLED ISLAND PILGRIMAGE

Slovenia's only island commands respect: a pilgrimage site for over 1000 years, the church castaway on Lake Bled is still worth the boat trip or swim.

For hundreds of years, the faithful have flocked to the teensy island at the west end of Slovenia's best-known lake to worship at the church that adorns it. Their motivations for doing so hark back over a millennium to a temple honouring the Slavic Goddess Živa on this site, which was subsequently built over by a succession of church buildings.

The baroque beauty that crests this tree-stippled cay now is every bit as much a pilgrimage destination as its predecessors, and it is arrestingly beautiful against a pin-up backdrop of Lake Bled with the Julian Alps soaring behind. But the getting there certainly whets your appetite for further exploring this body of water. For the last few centuries, pilgrims have traditionally been ferried over the few-hundred-metres crossing by *pletna* – a flat-bottomed wooden boat – and this is still possible. Or you could hire your own rowboat. Or you could swim.

Country Slovenia · **Type** lake · **Cost** Return *pletna* boat €15 per person, one-hour boat hire €15, swimming free · **Activities** boat tour, wild swimming · **Family friendly** yes

Why swim if I can take a boat?

Swimming is free. It's also more original, and then you are not tied to boat schedules. It is also something of a rite-of-passage activity among Slovenia-bound adventurers. A word of warning, though: your swimming costume is not deemed sufficient clothing to enter a Catholic place of worship. So make sure you arrange for someone else to bring your garments if you want to go inside the church, or swim with a dry bag containing your towel and attire.

Where do I take a boat from / swim from?

Pletna boats leave from Cesta Svobode, near the junction with Mlinska Cesta on the southern lakeshore southeast of the island. Rowboats can be rented from a few locations, including one on the shoreline directly west of the island on Kidričeva Cesta. Want to swim? It will help your cause if you set out from the shore close to Villa Bled on the southern lakeshore, probably the nearest point to the island.

Be 'oar-struck' by its beauty ~ Pilgrimage church with its backdrop of the Julian Alps ~ Forgo the rowboat and swim instead ~ The cool water tempts after the sweaty stair climb

The Wishing Bell

A bell in the church, dating to 1534, supposedly grants one wish to those who ring it. It was not always so fortunate for those who encountered a church bell. During transportation of the Wishing Bell's predecessor, a storm sunk the boat and crew. This unlucky bell tolls still, they say.

PUNTA PALOMA

A perfect salt-white dune, world-renowned wave-riding and views of Morocco await at one of Spain's most fabulous swaths of coast.

The southern Spanish region of Andalucía pulls in a staggering 10 million visitors a year, most of them on the hunt for sunny beachside bliss. Those in the know make straight for the wind-lashed, all-natural throwback of Cádiz province's ravishing Costa de la Luz, where the dusty cream-coloured beaches sprinkled around the ancient, kitesurfing-mad town of Tarifa evoke all that's wonderful about this unspoilt, boho-feel patch of Spain.

At locally loved Punta Paloma, a pale-gold dune cascades down from a pine-studded hillside to meet the aquamarine Atlantic Ocean, with Morocco glinting just across the water and the kites of wave-riders speckling the horizon – this is one of Andalucía's (and Spain's) most exquisite beaches. Don't miss the help-yourself natural mud bath at its northern end; you can rinse off by plunging back into the Atlantic waves, before tucking into a crunchy homemade *bocadillo* (filled roll).

Country Spain · **Region** Tarif, Costa de la Luz · **Type** beach · **Activities** swimming, kitesurfing, windsurfing, walking, horse riding · **Family friendly** yes

Beach bliss with views stretching out to Morocco

Isn't the breeze a bit inconvenient?
Sometimes! But don't let that put you off – there's still plenty to enjoy when the wind picks up, including the sight of kitesurfers and windsurfers zipping across the waves.

Is everyone here for the water sports?
Not at all – Punta Paloma's powdery sands are just as popular with tribes of swimmers and sun-soakers, and the main kitesurfing/ windsurfing action happens on neighbouring Playa de Valdevaqueros.

How's the water?
While it's true that the Atlantic can often be rougher and chillier than the Mediterranean, this is still a heavenly spot for a dip. The sea is at its warmest in August and September (around 23°C/73°F).

Once I'm done relaxing on the beach, what else is there to do?
You can walk along the coast, beyond the mud baths, to the seaside Roman ruins at Bolonia; or head to one of the low-key *chiringuitos* (beach bars) dotted between Punta Paloma and Tarifa town.

207

Kitesurfing & Windsurfing Schools

For those wanting to ride Tarifa's waves, reputable schools include Gisela Pulido Pro Center, started by a world kitesurfing champion, and well-established Spin Out, with a branch on Valdevaqueros. May, June and September have the best conditions for beginners.

YSTRADFELLTE WATERFALLS

These fifteen idyllic cascades, most accessible to the public, lace woodsy ravines around the Welsh village of Ystradfellte.

Everything you ever wanted to do at a waterfall, pretty much, can be done at the cascades around the village of Ystradfellte. Several of the most iconic falls – Sgwd Uchaf Clun-Gwyn, Sgwd Isaf Clun-Gwyn, Sgwd y Pannwr and Sgwd-yr-Eira – are incorporated into the Four Waterfalls Walk, a well-marked 8km (5-mile) circular trail.

Heading anticlockwise, first up is the ferocious Sgwd Uchaf Clun-Gwyn. It is more for gawking at in awe, although off-piste paths lead off the main trail near here to some superb fast-flowing stretches of river suitable for a paddle. Sgwd Isaf Clun-Gwyn may be the least dramatic, but its gurgling mini-falls and plunge pools have the best swimming. Sgwd y Pannwr, tumbling wide over low foliage-clad cliffs, has a wonderful spread-out area below for splash-abouts. And at the final fall, Sgwd-yr-Eira, plummeting in picture-perfect satin sheets, you can clamber behind the cascades to the opposite riverbank.

Country Wales • **Region** Powys • **Type** waterfalls • **Activities** wild swimming, hiking, caving • **Family friendly** yes

Hikers are rewarded with impressive waterfalls and plunge pools to cool off in

What is Waterfall Country?

Ystradfellte's celebrated cascades are part of a wider area around the head of the Vale of Neath known for its high concentration of waterfalls: this is often collectively called 'Waterfall Country'. As well as the Mellte and the Hepste, visited on the Four Waterfalls Walk, the other fall-rich rivers hereabouts include the Afon Pyrddin and Nedd Fechan. The highest falls in South Wales, Henrhyd Falls (27m/90ft) are also in Waterfall Country, on the Nant Llech river.

Which is the best part of the Four Waterfalls Walk to get in the water?

Sgwd Isaf Clun-Gwyn's falls and pools have quite a few areas to get safely down to the water's edge and in for a swim without the current posing a threat.

Are there any refreshments around here?

In the main car parks of Cwm Porth and Gwaun Hepste, there is often an ice-cream or snack van during summer months.

Caving

Aside from its watery delights, Ystradfellte is also special because of its spelunking. Best-known among these subterranean thrills is Porth yr Ogof, with Wales' widest cave entrance among the 15-odd ways into its 2.5km (1.5-mile) extent. Water, in the guise of the rushing River Mellte, intensifies the caving challenges within.

ELAFONISI BEACH

In a remote pocket of Crete's southwestern corner, aquamarine waters swirl with pastel-pink sands to create a magical lagoon beach.

Crete is well known for having a clutch of beautiful beaches spread out across the island, and while it might be tough to pick a standout, Elafonisi is certainly up there. Situated in a hidden pocket of the island's southwest, it impresses sun-seekers who have made the trip out here with its undeniable raw beauty. A natural phenomenon, caused by crushed shells washing up over the years onto the shore, has turned its sandy beach into a pretty melange of dusky pink and white grains with clear turquoise waters shimmering over the top.

The lagoon-beach's shallow warm waters are ideal for families to splash around in and also keep the Instagram crowd happy with perfect selfie scenes. To escape the crowds and find a patch of your own Elafonisi paradise, head past the lagoon and sunbed-covered main beach to explore the dunes and hidden coves of Elafonisi islet further along.

Country Greece · **Region** Crete · **Type** beach · **Family friendly** yes

What are the facilities like here?

Fairly basic. There isn't really a town at Elafonisi, just a few hotels spread out and a couple of basic restaurants attached to the hotels, and the beach, that's it. There are toilets you can use for a small fee and several snack stands selling food and drink at the beach. For a more substantial feed, head up the road a short walk to the laid-back restaurant at Elafonisi Resort.

Is there any shade at the beach?

Umbrellas and sun loungers can be hired for a fee.

Where can I stay?

There are a couple of accommodation options on the main road before you hit the path down to the beach, including Elafonisi Resort which has some budget rooms and lovely modern studios set in an olive grove.

What can I do when I'm tired of lazing on the beach?

Hop in the car (it's best to have your own wheels to get here) and head 5km (3.1 miles) north to the beautiful seaside Hrysoskalitissas Monastery.

Magical colours of Elafonisi Beach ~ Impressively clear water you won't be able to resist ~ The shallow lagoon is perfect for wading ~ Escape the crowds to your own private patch on the islet

Kedrodasos Beach

If the crowds at Elafonisi are too much, seek out Kedrodasos beach just 1km (0.6 miles) east of Elafonisi. You reach it via a 2.5km (1.5-mile) dirt road lined with greenhouses to the car park, then a short walk down a rocky path. It's backed by forest and has a beautiful arc of white sand, and it's popular with nudists.

© Janelle Lugge | Getty Images

OCEANIA

JELLYFISH LAKE

Swim, or just float, in a hidden lake that's so full of non-stinging jellyfish that it feels like you're bathing in blancmange.

Palau's Rock Islands create some of the most magnificent and distinctive ocean-scapes anywhere on this beautiful blue planet. Seen from the air, it's as though an exuberant artist has squirted green oil-paint in thick, random squiggles onto a dazzling turquoise canvas. Approached by boat, what you see are lush dwarf forests overhanging their coral islet homes on coastlines curiously undercut by wave erosion. As if sailing through this environment weren't special enough, in the middle of one such islet is a unique lake in which jellyfish have survived for so long with no predators that they have lost their sting. While populations oscillate according to climate variations, there are usually so many of the delicate, harmless creatures gathered at one side of the lake, that when you dive in it feels like there's more jelly than water. Swimming through this mass of soft, alien life is an unforgettable tactile experience.

Country Palau · **Region** Eil Malik Island · **Type** lake · **Cost** permit US$100; only accessible by boat · **Activities** gentle swimming · **Family Friendly** yes, for older kids

A snorkelling sight to behold ~ Walk the dock and jump on in ~ Don't worry, these jellyfish are harmless ~ Views over Palau's Rock Islands

Are you sure I won't get stung?
If you weren't nervous about touching jellyfish, you'd be pretty warped. But here, once you've brushed past a few, you'll relax into the experience.

What if I can't find the jellyfish?
You're on the wrong side of the lake: the 'swarm' moves around following the sun.

How do I get here?
Boat tours operate from Koror, the capital of Palau – a small Pacific island nation that's most conveniently reached from the Philippines. Visits are often combined with scuba diving trips to Palau's magnificent blue-holes and drop-offs.

Will I need snorkelling equipment?
Yes...so that you see as well as feel what you're swimming through, and to better appreciate the magical forms of the little beings.

How fit should I be?
The swimming itself is little more demanding than taking a bath. You can reach the lake from the jetty via cement steps and guide ropes.

Jellyfish Population

The lake was closed for a couple of years after a drought caused a catastrophic collapse in jellyfish numbers. This happens occasionally but the population has since recovered and tours resumed in 2019.

BAY OF FIRES

Orange-lichen-covered boulders plonked on white beaches lapped by glass-clear waters give this beautiful bay an otherworldly atmosphere.

Extending along Tasmania's east coast from Binalong Bay in the south to Eddystone Point at the northern end, larapuna/Bay of Fires is a sight to behold. Its string of spectacular, often secluded, beaches offer dazzling, clear waters and sugar-white sands punctuated with granite boulders splashed with vivid-orange-coloured lichen. It might be tempting to spend hours simply taking in the surreal views, but there are plenty of activities here to keep you occupied, from kayaking and surfing to diving and fishing. Be warned though: these waters are breathtakingly chilly most of the year.

The relaxed beach town of Binalong Bay has a gorgeous stretch of beach that's good for swimming and for surfing around the bay. Otherwise, head out on the water with Bay of Fires Eco Tours for a chance to spot dolphins, learn about Aboriginal sites and witness the true beauty of some of the remote parts of this magnificent coast.

Country Australia · **Region** Tasmania · **Type** bay ·
Activities available swimming, boating, diving, fishing, hiking · **Family friendly** yes

Keep an eye out for cute wallabies ~ You are now leaving Binalong Bay ~ Plenty of hikes to take advantage of ~ Bright orange lichen blankets the boulders

When is the best time to go?

The Bay of Fires is good for exploring at any time of the year, though it transitions from sleepy and secluded to a hive of activity over summer (December to February). The water temperature warms up, slightly, around March and April, and the summer crowds disappear.

Where can I stay?

If you're looking for luxury, the Bay of Fires Lodge is it. Featuring lots of Tasmanian hardwood and big glass windows, the eco-lodge is set on a hilltop surrounded by national park and with fantastic views. Otherwise, there are plenty of free camping spots and houses for rent in the region.

Are there any good walks in the area?

Absolutely, it's one of the main activities here. The ultimate walk is the four-day, three-night guided Bay of Fires Lodge walk. It starts at Mt William National Park and includes a day of kayaking as well as beach camping, along with a couple of nights staying at the Bay of Fires Lodge itself.

What's in a Name?

With all those boulders covered in fiery orange lichen dotting the coast, it's easy to think they must have been the inspiration for the name, Bay of Fires. In fact, British explorer Tobias Furneaux named it in 1773 after sighting the smoke from the fires of the Aboriginal people, who know the area as larapuna.

LIMU POOLS

Surrounded by the endless blue of the South Pacific, the tiny Polynesian country of Niue is home to the sheltered and superbly scenic Limu Pools.

On one of the South Pacific's more remote and laid-back island nations, the crystalline pools at Limu are the most spectacular of the sea caves and natural swimming holes dotting Niue's dramatic uplifted coral atoll coastline.

A sturdy staircase descends through the shade of tropical rainforest to a pair of natural pools fringed by forested shards of indigo coral. One pool, replenished by Niue's subterranean water table, is wonderfully sheltered, while in the other pool colder fresh water mixes with warmer saltwater rolling in from the open sea to create a strange phenomenon. Where the flows combine, the water resembles fractured glass, and when viewed through a diving mask it's like swimming through a liquid ice cube. And with a maximum of around 200 tourists on Niue at any one time and an island population of just 1600, experiencing Limu is usually wonderfully private.

Country Niue • **Town** Namukulu village • **Type** natural pools • **Activities** snorkelling, swimming • **Family friendly** yes

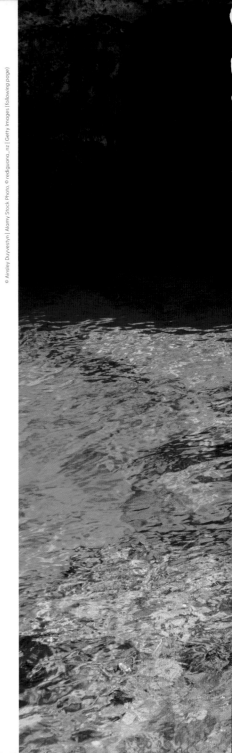

Swim your way through this wonderfully scenic sea cave

THE JOY OF WATER

Sounds amazing, how do I get here?
Just jump on an Air New Zealand plane from Auckland. The journey is less than four hours and there are a couple of flights a week. Too easy.

And I guess the water's really warm?
Depends really. Where it's coming from an underground spring it's pretty refreshing, but the ocean water's usually much warmer. Either way, it's perfect for cooling down in the tropical weather.

What about marine life? Is there much to see?
Definitely ask your guesthouse for a mask and snorkel. Tropical fish of all sizes and colours mooch around Limu's sheltered cove. Humpback whales visit to calve in Niue's warm waters from around June to September.

What about sandy beaches? It's a tropical South Pacific island, right?
Actually there are only a couple of tiny beaches on Niue. The real fun is exploring the pools and caverns around the coastline.

Seek Out
More Sea Caves

Rent a car to explore and to get
around to Niue's other spectacular sea
caves. Framed by high cliffs, Matapa
Chasm is where Niue's high-born chiefs
used to bathe. Named after the legendary
ancestral homeland of all Polynesians,
Avaiki Cave is sheltered from the
ocean and dappled with light
and shadows.

BELL GORGE

In the scorched heart of Australia's vast Kimberley region, the refreshing waters of Bell Gorge have soothed the parched bones of many a weary traveller.

You've been following the rough, dust-filled corrugations of the Kimberley's infamous Gibb River Road for days and the jarring bumps, insane heat and relentless flies are taking their toll. Relax, paradise is at hand! Deep in the Wilinggin Country of the Ngarinyin people, the natural amphitheatre and swimming hole of Bell Gorge is the perfect spot to cool off and break up that epic road trip.

A pleasant, partially shaded walk leads from the car park along a pandanus- and paperbark-fringed creek alive with birdsong. Breathtaking views from the top of the waterfall only hasten your pace to reach the cool, crystal waters below. Before long you're floating on your back (possibly still fully clothed) as you soak away the kilometres, staring up at the blue, cloudless sky and the sheer orange walls of the gorge. Yep, flat out, like that goanna on the rock to your right.

Country Australia • **Region** Western Australia • **Type** natural pool • **Cost** A$13 per car national park entry fee • **Activities** swimming, bushwalking • **Family friendly** yes

What's best about swimming here?
Getting up under the bottom of the falls and letting them pummel your back, best massage ever!

What's that stripey lizard over there?
That fella's a Mertens' water monitor, a type of goanna. Don't worry, they're harmless, as long as you leave them alone.

Near the cliffs above the falls, what was that pigeon that made a funny sound as it flew?
Big brown one? Yeah that's the white-quilled rock pigeon, they look just like the sandstone cliffs where they hide.

And that cute little purple-headed bird in the pandanus by the creek?
Oh you're lucky to see him. Purple-crowned fairy wren. Only the males get that purple colour when they're ready to breed; they're normally hiding in that pandanus.

Wow, I thought I just saw something jump along that cliff ledge?
Ha, you just saw a rock wallaby (like a little kangaroo), they hang out in the gorges and aren't afraid of heights!

Dramatic scenery everywhere you look ~ Leafy foliage springs from the gorge ~ Helicopter flights offer spectacular views ~ Sheer cliffs rise up from the swimming hole

Other Great Kimberley Swimming Gorges

Emma Gorge Possibly the prettiest plunge pool in the East Kimberley.

Galvans Gorge Right by the Gibb, lily-fringed and protected by a *wandjina* (powerful Indigenous rock-art figure).

Sir John Gorge Lovely water, and the red rocks turn the colour of molten lava at sunset.

DRIFT RIVER SNORKELLING

Meet platypuses, turtles and tropical fish while following the flow of a river through the Daintree Rainforest towards the Great Barrier Reef.

The quality of Queensland's aquatic riches is no secret, and donning a mask and fins to explore the salty coastscape is a popular pastime in Australia's Sunshine State, but the thrill of inland river snorkelling is a more secret buzz. Those who have goggled the gin-clear, freshwater flow of the Mossman River, amid the fantastic fecundity of the Daintree Rainforest, will never forget the experience.

This guided escapade sees small groups of wetsuit-clad adventurers drift along the river, spotting tropical fish, turtles, birdlife and even the occasional playful platypus. To gaze at a feature or fish for longer, you're taught to grab a rock and stay anchored for a spell. And when you want to chill out and effortlessly float, you can hop aboard your inflatable river sledge. As you go with the flow, your learned leader explains the relationship the river has with Queensland's Great Barrier Reef, as it supplies nutrients for the coral.

Country Australia • **Region** North Queensland • **Type** river • **Website** www.backcountrybliss.com.au • **Cost** A$105/90/360 per adult/child/family • **Family friendly** yes

© Jason Heffernan (right & following page)

Get acquainted with Australia's marine life on a river snorkelling trip

River swimming in Tropical North Queensland...will I not get eaten by crocodiles?
The section of the Mossman River explored during this experience is too clear, too cold, and too shaded for crocodiles – cold-blooded creatures that like to hide in warm, murky conditions. Don't make such assumptions for yourself, though, only swim with an expert.

What in the wild wet world is a river sledge?
It's a fancy name for a lilo – an inflatable device you can climb atop and float along the river on.

If this is the tropics, do I really need to wear a wetsuit?
Yeah – it helps with buoyancy, sun protection, and the water is surprisingly fresh at around 16 to 22°C (61 to 71.5°F).

Can I do this trip independently?
Given the presence of crocs – measuring up to 5m (16.4ft) in some parts of the Daintree – plus other hazards, it's potentially life-threatening to explore any stretch of water here unless you know it intimately. Go with those in the know.

"As our small group was drift-snorkelling down the river, we reached a spot known for platypus sightings. A young girl – eight or nine years old – popped her head up and said a platypus had been swimming alongside her. The joy on her face was priceless!"

Backcountry Bliss owner/head guide, Jason Heffernan

BONDI ICEBERGS CLUB

Overlooking Bondi Beach, Icebergs looks like an exclusive private club. But it's just the opposite – a community pool reminding Sydneysiders to relax.

Founded in 1929 by a group of Bondi Beach surf lifesavers who wanted to stay fit over winter, the Bondi Icebergs Winter Swimming Club started with a tin clubhouse that gradually expanded to a multistorey complex with one of the best views in Sydney. Despite its jaw-dropping location, Icebergs has retained a real sense of community, a grounding influence in a suburb that has been known to take itself a little bit too seriously.

There are two pools here – one 50m (164ft) Olympic-sized pool with lap lanes and one splash-about kids' pool – and plenty of space to relax in the sun. The rocky surrounds are painted white to resemble an iceberg. There's also a popular sauna (included in the entry fee), and in winter many swimmers dash between the sauna and the water to get their blood pumping with the change in temperature.

Country Australia · **City** Sydney · **Type** ocean pool · **Website** www.icebergs.com.au · **Cost** A$8/5.50 adult/child · **Activities** pool, sauna, yoga, gym · **Family friendly** yes

The ocean crashes into the iconic pool ~ Icebergs members hanging out ~ Drop in to the Bondi Pavilion

If it's called Icebergs it must be pretty cold?
It depends – it goes down to around 17°C (63°F) in winter and hits about 21°C (70°F) in summer. The club members are famous for swimming with chunks of ice, but it's really not that bad.

When do the club members swim?
They meet every Sunday – members have to swim three Sundays out of four all through winter. There's a kids' club too, called the Ice Cubes.

It sounds pretty hard-core. Do you have to be a strong swimmer to feel comfortable?
It's pretty relaxed. There's a slow lane and faster lanes. A few people there can swim pretty well, but it doesn't have the competitive vibe of the city pools. Except in the mornings with the before-work crowd.

Does the surf ever get into the pool?
Oh yeah. On good days, the surf washes into the pool, which makes it lots of fun. Big waves come crashing over your head and everything gets frothy and it's great.

"I like Icebergs, you can get into your laps because there are lanes. It's a proper 50m (164ft) Olympic swimming pool, unlike most of the other ocean pools where in summer it's a free-for-all of kids and paddlers and everyone else cutting you off."

Bob Scott,
local Icebergs swimmer

MATARANKA THERMAL POOL

The Australian Outback can be notoriously forbidding, but not at Mataranka, where thermal pools fold visitors into a warm and wet embrace.

Just over an hour by car from Katherine and easily visited as a day trip, the little township of Mataranka has secured its place on the map through its sandy-bottomed thermal pools in natural settings, surrounded by cabbage palm and paperbark trees.

There are only two swimmable pools: Bitter Springs, which was found by telegraph line surveyors in the 19th century and is now located within the boundaries of Elsey National Park, and the larger Mataranka Thermal Pool. Remember: it's always smart to respect the swimming signs, since saltwater crocodiles inhabit the nearby Roper River.

The pools' gloriously clear, spring-fed, mineral-rich waters come bubbling out of the ground – at more than 30°C (86°F) in the case of the Mataranka Thermal Pool – and certainly carry medicinal reward, but it's the emotional boost from the surrounding environment, often including flying foxes, that truly inspires.

Country Australia • **Region** Northern Territory • **Type** hot springs • **Family friendly** yes

When should I visit?
The pools are open all year-round, but the most popular time of year is May to October. That's when the days are warm and dry, but the nights still get cool.

What should I bring?
Everything that you'll need, especially a swimsuit and towel. Since these are natural outdoor springs, a hat, sunscreen, bug repellent and drinkable water are also pretty key.

Do I have to walk to the springs?
In each case, there is an easy 500m (1640ft) loop path that leads right by. That said, there are also longer hikes in the adjacent national park.

Is there more to Mataranka than the thermal springs and hikes?
There's the Never Never Museum, the Elsey Homestead Replica and some interesting WWII history, including an Aboriginal army camp just south of Mataranka township.

Take a break from the Outback heat ~ Stunning scenery surrounds the pool ~ Red flying foxes might swing by

We of the Never Never

As showcased in the local Never Never Museum, Australian writer Jeannie Gunn published *We of the Never Never* in 1908, a classic autobiographical novel about the hardships of early 20th-century life in the Australian Outback. She wrote about Elsey Station, near Mataranka, making the town and its hot springs famous.

NINGALOO REEF

Dive down under the Ningaloo Reef to come face-to-face with some of Australia's most awesome marine life – whale sharks, manta rays and turtles.

Shoals of electric-blue damselfish, yellow-ribboned sweetlips and iridescent parrotfish swirl like tropical storm clouds, flitting in and out of rocky enclaves. A blissed-out loggerhead turtle beats time with the ocean as it glides over an underwater forest of staghorn coral and neon-bright sponges – totally oblivious to you spluttering into your snorkel. You find Nemo: a clownfish playing peek-a-boo in the tentacles of a sea anemone. And just when you think it can't get any more mind-blowing, manta rays rock up, flying carpets of the deep with dance moves and 7m (23ft) wingspans that elicit bubbles of excitement.

Welcome to Ningaloo, one of the world's largest and most accessible fringing coral reefs, unravelling some 5000 sq km (1930 sq miles) off the mid-west coast of Western Australia. The Great Barrier Reef gets all the fuss, but this Unesco World Heritage marine park is every bit as awesome.

Country Australia · **Region** Western Australia · **Type** coral reef · **Cost** excursion costs vary · **Activities** swimming, snorkelling, scuba diving, kayaking · **Family friendly** yes

Get up close with a majestic whale shark at one of the world's largest coral reefs

How do I reach Ningaloo?
Like much of Western Australia, the Ningaloo Reef is pretty remote, which is part of its beauty. Qantas operates daily flights from Perth to Learmonth Airport, Exmouth – a fine base for exploring the reef.

What's the marine life like?
Sensational. Some 500 species of fish, as well as turtles, manta rays, dugongs, whales, whale sharks and dolphins splash around in the Indian Ocean.

Snorkel or dive?
Spotting marine life is often as simple as popping on a snorkel and sticking your head under. Diving, naturally, takes you deeper. Dive centres offer courses and rent out equipment around Coral Bay and Exmouth.

What's the best way to explore?
While you can easily hook onto a day's excursion, Sail Ningaloo's super-stylish live-aboard catamaran gets you properly out on the reef, with unlimited snorkelling and diving at hidden sites. Tours have impeccable eco credentials.

Marine Life Highs

Time your trip to swim alongside the world's biggest fish – the whale shark – from mid-March to July, when these humongous filter feeders flock here to feast on krill during coral spawning season. From July to October, migratory humpback whales use the reef as a giant nursery.

WHITEHAVEN BEACH

Pack your sunglasses – you're going to need them when you take in the view of this 7km (4-mile) stretch of some of the whitest sand in the world.

Australia is known for having some of the best beaches on the planet, and Whitehaven Beach on the Whitsunday Islands is testament to that. This stunner, backed by velvety green forest, dazzles those fortunate enough to set eyes on it, with swirling azure waters lapping at blinding white sand that just begs for a bit of toe sinking – at 98% silica, it's baby-powder soft.

The Whitsundays – a string of 74 islands located off the coast of Queensland – are a popular playground with all manner of water-based activities. Here you can choose to stay dry and set sail on the calm, tropical waters sheltered by the Great Barrier Reef or strap on a snorkel to discover what's under that brilliant, blue sea. But the one thing visitors here wouldn't dream of missing out on is the chance to step foot on this near-mythical pristine beach.

Country Australia · **Region** Queensland · **Type** beach · **Activities** swimming, sailing · **Family Friendly** yes

Sailing the Whitsunday seas ~ Get an aerial view on seaplane ride ~ Whale-watching season is from June to September ~ One of the world's best beaches

So there are 74 islands in the Whitsundays, which one is Whitehaven Beach on?
The beach is located on the largest island called Whitsunday Island.

How do I reach it?
Tour operators arrange trips from Airlie Beach, the mainland gateway to the islands. Otherwise, if you're staying at one of the handful of resort islands (Daydream Island, Hamilton Island, etc), you can arrange a day-trip excursion through the resort.

I've seen amazing aerial shots of the beach, how do I get that view?
Various operators can get you up in the sky in a seaplane or helicopter on a scenic flight over the Great Barrier Reef and Whitehaven Beach.

Is it possible to camp on the beach?
Yes, at the southern end, but you'll need to bring essentials (drinking water, food, rubbish bags) and have your own boat to get here. There are basic toilet facilities, and no fires are permitted.

Stinger Season

The high-risk season for jellyfish in the Whitsundays is from October to May. The two main types here are the tiny Irukandji and the box jellyfish. While rare, the Irukandji sting can be fatal, as can the box jellyfish if the sting is substantial enough. Reputable tour operators will provide 'stinger suits' for customers.

AITUTAKI LAGOON

Snorkel, kitesurf or simply float around in a crystal-clear Pacific-island lagoon that honeymoons are made of.

Aitutaki means 'a little paradise', and the name couldn't be more apt for this small Pacific archipelago encircled by a huge lagoon widely considered to be the world's most beautiful. Crystal-clear, warm water and shallow depths – averaging 5m (16ft) – together with steady winds make the breathtaking turquoise lagoon an ideal place to learn how to kitesurf, but that's just one of the many activities available. Among the most popular options is to sign up for a snorkelling tour by boat, which takes in some of the 14 tiny *motu*, islets that curl around the eastern fringe of the lagoon. You can also rent a kayak, book a scuba-diving trip to the outer reef, or simply lounge around on the sparkling white sand in front of your resort.

Country Cook Islands • **Region** Aitutaki island • **Type** natural lagoon • **Activities** swimming, snorkelling, kayaking, kitesurfing, scuba diving • **Family friendly** yes

Paradise on Earth ~ Incredibly clear waters make snorkelling a breeze ~ Colourful fish dart around

© ChameleonsEye | Shutterstock, © Dirk Freder | Getty Images, © Ray Hems | Getty Images, © Andrea Izzotti | Shutterstock (following page)

How do I get here?
Aitutaki is a 50-minute flight from the main island, Rarotonga. Air Rarotonga also offers day trips to Aitutaki from the main island.

Where should I stay?
There's no 'bad' spot to stay on the main island, with most accommodation options lining the west coast.

Is the snorkelling any good?
As the bottom of the lagoon is mostly sandy, you'll need to jump on a lagoon boat tour to access the best snorkelling spots.

Are there sharks in the lagoon?
Sharks are only very rarely sighted in the lagoon. You're much more likely to spot a turtle, along with loads of colourful giant clams on the coral bombies.

Is there much else to do on Aitutaki?
Yes, you can learn about the island's history and culture on a Punarei Cultural Tour, led by locals.

Stay in Style

Consider splurging on a stay at Aitutaki Lagoon Private Resort, the only resort with direct access to the lagoon. It's also the only overwater bungalow accommodation across the Cook Islands, complete with suitably romantic Polynesian-inspired bungalows.

ABEL TASMAN NATIONAL PARK

Be wowed by crescent-shaped bays, bottle-green waters and dolphin encounters as you swim, paddle and camp in the coastal Abel Tasman NP.

Imagine the delirious delight of salt-bedraggled Dutch explorer Abel Tasman when he clapped eyes on the shores of New Zealand back in 1642. Like travellers today, he was no doubt stunned by the beauty of the northern tip of the South Island, as frankly few coastlines on earth can compete. Going slow here – on foot or by kayak – is the *only* way to go, and thank heavens for that.

Immune to time and trends, the 60km (37-mile) Coast Track takes you up and over hills draped in sun-dappled native beech forest and over crystal-clear streams that run to half-moon bays of ochre-gold sand and jade-green water. Water is a constant: whether you're swimming in a secluded cove, paddling in quiet exhilaration around a marine reserve where dolphins and seals frolic, or listening to the gently lapping sea beneath an expansive night sky stitched with layers of stars.

Country New Zealand · **Region** South Island · **Type** coastal park · **Cost** entry free, activities vary · **Activities** swimming, kayaking, hiking, canyoning, sailing · **Family Friendly** yes

The aptly named Split Apple Rock ~ Dangle over the treetops ~ Seals splashing around ~ Kayakers take to the waters

How can I access the Coast Track?
Taking three to five days, the south-to-north Coast Track runs from Marahau to Wainui Bay. As it's not a circular trail, you'll need to arrange a shuttle or water taxi at either end.

Where can I stay?
There are four huts with bunkrooms, toilets and washbasins plus 21 campsites. All must be pre-booked at https://bookings.doc.govt.nz.

What should I bring?
Everything. You'll need a backpack, tent, cooking stove, torch, sturdy shoes, bathing suit, waterproofs, sunscreen and mosquito repellent. Some huts have filtered drinking water, but bring all food.

When's best to go?
Most people go in summer (October to April) but insiders say the shoulder seasons are more peaceful, with calm waters and quiet beaches.

How about kayaking?
Reputable companies including Abel Tasman Kayaks offer guided kayaking excursions.

Cleopatra's Pool

Well hidden and worth seeking out,
Cleopatra's Pool is a short detour off
the Coast Track between Torrent Bay and
Anchorage. The trail passes through lush,
mossy, fern-flecked woods to emerge at
an incredible rock pool with a natural
waterslide. The slide is a fairly smooth
ride but wear waterproof shoes
for the rocks at the bottom.

TO SUA OCEAN TRENCH

Clamber down the wooden ladder to float in Samoa's most Instagrammed natural swimming hole.

With its rugged volcanic coastline lapped by idyllic turquoise waters, Samoa isn't short of incredible swimming spots. But just off the main coast road of the nation's main island, Upolu, lies a swimming hole to rule them all. Rimmed by lush, green vegetation, To Sua, or 'big hole with water coming out of it', consists of two large holes in an ancient lava field connected by a lava tunnel.

Accessed by a bamboo ladder, the larger hole is a blissful spot for a soak in the sparkling, clear water, with the pool fed by a series of canals and tunnels with water from the ocean pounding just metres away. The bottom (if you can reach it) is sandy, and there's a rope to hold onto when the tidal surge is strong. It's also possible to swim through the short, semi-submerged lava tunnel to the tiny beach at the base of the smaller hole.

Country Samoa • **Region** Upolu island • **Type** natural pool • **Cost** ST20 • **Family Friendly** yes, though close supervision is required for younger children

First you must climb down the ladder ~ The cordyline plant brightens things up ~ A sign marks the entrance ~ Splash down in the trench

Is it as amazing as it looks on Instagram?
In a word – yes. Though keep in mind that you will need to be here at the 8.30am opening time for the best chance of enjoying it all to yourself.

Could I be sucked out to sea?
There have been tales of swimmers being sucked through the underwater tunnels to the ocean. If there's a strong current, hold onto the rope tightly and keep your distance from the side of the trench closest to the ocean.

Is there anything else to do here?
Don't leave the site without taking a stroll around the stunning coastline just beyond the trench. Better yet, bring a packed lunch and hang out at one of the picnic tables for the day.

Play it Safe

Gorgeous as it is here, visitors still need to exercise caution: the ladder can be slippery, and attempting to swim through the underwater passage that feeds the waterhole is incredibly dangerous. Travelling with kids? Beware the child-sized gaps in the fence that encircles the top of the trench.

INDEX

The Joy of Water

May 2020

Published by Lonely Planet Global Limited

CRN 554153

www.lonelyplanet.com

10 9 8 7 6 5 4 3 2 1

Printed in Singapore

ISBN 978 18386 9046 5

© Lonely Planet 2020

© photographers as indicated 2020

Managing Director, Publishing Piers Pickard

Associate Publisher Robin Barton

Commissioning Editor Kate Morgan

Art Director Daniel Di Paolo

Designer & image researcher Lauren Egan

Proof reader Bridget Blair

Writers: Abigail Blasi, Brett Atkinson, Celeste Brash, Christina Webb, Dinah Gardner, Emily Matchar, Ethan Gelber, Greg Benchwick, Helena Smith, Isabella Noble, Joe Bindloss, Joe Davis, Joel Balsam, Kate Morgan, Kerry Christiani; Luke Waterson, Mark Elliot, Monique Perrin, Oliver Berry, Patrick Kinsella, Raymond Bartlett, Sarah Reid, Stephen Lioy, Steve Waters, Tasmin Waby

Cover image of Capri: © Seth Willingham / www.waterprojectphoto.com

Lonely Planet Offices

Australia

The Malt Store, Level 3,

551 Swanston St, Carlton, Victoria 3053

T: 03 8379 8000

USA

Suite 208, 155 Filbert Street,

Oakland, CA 94607

T: 510 250 6400

Ireland

Digital Depot, Roe Lane (off Thomas St),

Digital Hub, Dublin 8,

D08 TCV4

Europe

240 Blackfriars Rd,

London SE1 8NW

T: 020 3771 5100

STAY IN TOUCH lonelyplanet.com/contact